P9-EKJ-994

Cross-Stitch from a Country Garden

from McCall's Needlework & Crafts

SEDGEWOOD® PRESS
New York

For Sedgewood® Press

Director: Elizabeth P. Rice
Editorial Project Manager: Susan A. Siegler
Project Editor: Margo Kaminsky
Production Manager: Bill Rose
Designer: H. Roberts

Distributed by Meredith Corporation, Des Moines, Iowa.

ISBN 0-696-02303-2
Library of Congress Catalog Card Number: 87-60952

Printed in the United States of America
10 9 8 7

Contents

Introduction

Even if you've never embroidered before, you can create a beautiful world of flowers, using just one simple stitch! Cross-stitch, the most basic of embroidery stitches, is easy to learn and virtually mistake-proof. All of the designs in this book are worked in what is called the "counted cross-stitch" method. That simply means you count the very visible threads of an even-weave fabric and stitch an "x" over them.

The chart for each design is merely a "paint by number" guide. Each symbol on the chart represents a different color; you "paint" that color with your needle and floss.

Once you have tried cross-stitch (actually, after the first two or three stitches, you'll be a pro!), you will realize how versatile the stitch can be. Because threads are counted for the placement of each stitch, the size of your finished design is determined by the number of threads per inch in your fabric. For instance, if you are stitching a flower over two threads on 14-threads-per-inch fabric, you will complete seven stitches in an inch. Using that same chart and stitch count on a coarser 6-threads-per-inch fabric, you will complete only three stitches in an inch. The flower on the coarser fabric will be more than twice as large as the first. You will have used the exact same chart to get two entirely different looks!

After you have browsed through our color-filled collection, take a closer look and see how the designs can be adapted for your own special use. The sampler shown on page 98 will give you some ideas for "designing your own" by using a portion of an existing design or a different thread count fabric. The sampler's center basket motif was quickly stitched on a set of coasters. The chrysanthemum-filled urn was embroidered on coarser fabric for a pillow's central motif, and the sampler's border was used to brighten a place mat. You can see the possibilities are endless!

We hope this book will guide you down the glorious garden path of cross-stitch, and we trust that your creative needs and love of beautiful things will be fulfilled by these designs and their yet-to-be-imagined possibilities.

ABCDE
FG HI
JK LM
N O
PQ RS
TU VW
XYZ MD

Fresh from the cutting garden...

Create everlasting bouquets of flowers that will remain as lovely as the day they were "clipped" from the garden.

- Alphabet Sampler with Carnations
- Basket of Wildflowers Patchwork
- Gazebo in a Flowering Garden
- Place Mats as Fresh as Spring
- Rose Wreath Tablecloth
- Tulip Time Trio
- Violet Trellis Basket
- Purple Iris Triptych
- Garden Potpourri Lids and Sachets

opposite page: Alphabet Sampler with Carnations

Alphabet Sampler with Carnations

This rosy pot of posies, adapted from an appliquéd quilt, is paired with an elegant alphabet for a unique sampler.

Sampler

SIZE:
$11\frac{3}{4}'' \times 17\frac{3}{4}''$.

EQUIPMENT:
Ruler. Pencil. Scissors. Embroidery hoop. Tapestry needle. Straight pins. Steam iron. Sewing machine (optional).

MATERIALS:
Zweigart® "Florina" (14-count) fabric, piece $14'' \times 20\frac{1}{2}''$; to order from Hansi's Haus, see Buyers' Guide, page 174. Persian yarn: 16 yards light rose, 24 yards dark rose. Illustration board, $11\frac{1}{2}'' \times 17\frac{1}{2}''$. Masking tape.

DIRECTIONS:
Read Cross-Stitch How-To's, page 177. Place fabric in hoop, making sure horizontal and vertical threads are straight and even; move hoop as needed.

Work design, following chart and color key. Each square on chart represents two horizontal and two vertical threads on fabric; each symbol represents one cross-stitch. Separate yarn and work with single strand in needle throughout. Work all letters (dots) in dark rose and entire flower motif (Xs) in light rose. Work all stitches over two threads in each direction.

To Stitch: With short fabric edges at top and bottom, measure 2″ down and in from upper left corner to correspond with upper left corner of chart; mark with a pin. Following chart, begin top of letter A by counting two threads down and four threads to the right, for first stitch. Work first row of alphabet. Work second row of alphabet, including top of central flower. Continue working letters and flower motif to end of chart. Work one or two of your own initials in the center of blank space at lower right corner. (It is best to plot out initial(s) in pencil on chart before embroidering.) Place finished embroidery, face down, on padded surface and steam-press lightly from center outward.

To Finish: Center illustration board on wrong side of stitched fabric; fold raw edges over board and tape in place. Frame as desired.

ALPHABET SAMPLER WITH CARNATIONS

☒ Light Rose
⊡ Dark Rose

Basket of Wildflowers Patchwork

"Basket of Wildflowers" combines cross-stitch and crewel embroidery stitches with patchwork to produce an heirloom-quality wall hanging or throw.

Wildflower Patchwork

SIZE:

Approximately 29¾″ square.

EQUIPMENT:

Ruler. Red pencil. Scissors. Basting thread. Tapestry needle. Sewing needle or sewing machine. Embroidery hoop. Steam iron. Stiff cardboard. Tracing paper. White glue. Quilting needle. Water-erasable marking pen.

MATERIALS:

White 14-count Fine Aida fabric 43″ wide, ½ yard. Susan Bates Anchor® six-strand embroidery floss, one skein each color listed in key, unless otherwise indicated in parentheses. Cotton fabrics 44″ wide: Pink floral, ⅞ yard; blue print, ½ yard; rose plaid, ¼ yard; ecru floral, ⅛ yard. White lightweight closely woven fabric, 12″ square, for interfacing. White and pink sewing thread. Batting. White quilting thread.

DIRECTIONS:

Read Patchwork How-To's, page 181, Embroidery Basics, page 175, and Cross-Stitch How-To's, page 177. Remember to pre-shrink cotton Aida fabric along with other fabrics before beginning stitchery.

Embroidery: Mark center block and borders on Aida as follows; mark along a row of holes and keep pieces 1″ from fabric edges and 1″ apart: For center block, mark an 18″ square. For borders, mark four 2½″ × 19½″ rectangles. On each marked shape, count to locate center row of holes both horizontally and vertically; baste along these holes using contrast-color thread (on borders, lengthwise center is row of threads—baste either side of this row). On charts, use a red pencil to connect horizontal and vertical lines indicated by arrows. Work embroidery in a hoop. Unless otherwise indicated, work with two strands of floss, cut to 18″ lengths. For stitch details, see page 178. Generally, work all cross-stitches first, then work backstitches along one fabric square, then work other embroidery stitches as indicated.

Center Block: Begin with Chart 1; start at intersection of basting stitches with center of chart. On iris centers, work long straight stitches, referring to chart for length of stitches and using three strands of floss; at the top end of each straight stitch, add a French knot. When Chart 1 has been followed completely, work airy floral sprigs on top following Chart 2. Dotted lines indicate design already in place; count cross-stitches to locate starting points for each sprig. Work backstitch stems first, then lazy daisy leaves, then bullion stitches, then pale salmon French knots in threesomes. Finally, scatter light cobalt blue French knots more or less randomly around sprigs. When all stitchery is completed, remove from hoop. Carefully measure out 8″ from center along each basted line; mark points with water-erasable pen. Connect points with diagonal lines, creating an 11″ square around design. Cut out, leaving ½″ seam allowance all around. Pin square face up on white lightweight cotton fabric with cut edges along the grain. Cut out lightweight fabric even with Aida. Baste along seam line through both layers, to interface Aida.

Borders: On each strip, count 5 stitches up from center (along the length) and start with upper rose at bottom of stem. Work stem in backstitch first, then work cross-stitches, then backstitches around flower, then French knots. Work lower flower, counting threads and squares on chart for positioning. Repeat entire design above and below this pair for a total of 6

(continued)

motifs; align stems with long basting stitches. Cut out ½″ beyond marked lines.

Patches: Add ½″ seam allowances to all pieces. Trace actual-size patterns and make templates for B, C, D, H, and I pieces. From rose plaid, cut 4 strips 1¼″ × 12⅜″ (A), 4 strips 1¼″ × 19½″ (E), and 8 rectangles 1¼″ × 2½″ (G). From pink floral fabric, cut out 4 B, 4 H. From blue print, cut 8 D. From ecru fabric, cut 16 C, 16 I, and 4 1¼″ squares (F).

Assemble Quilt Top: Piecing diagram shows ¼ of quilt. Arrange all pieces on a large, flat surface. First, arrange all patches according to diagram, to form upper right quarter of quilt top. Rotate chart ¼ turn clockwise and arrange patches for lower right quarter, repeat to arrange lower left and upper left quarters.

First, frame center embroidery block with A strips, working clockwise in a log-cabin pattern: Pin an A to block as shown in piecing diagram, with one short edge flush with side corner of block, other short edge extending past top corner. Stitch. Pin, then stitch second A strip across flush short edge plus lower right edge of block. Add third strip A across short edge and lower left side of quilt block. Add fourth strip across upper left edge; slip-stitch short edge to fit extension of first A strip. Framed block should measure 13¾″ square inside seam allowances.

Stitch a C patch to each side of B patches, forming a square, 4⅞″ inside seam allowances. Stitch a D patch to two adjacent sides of this square, forming a triangle, with longest edge 13¾″ inside seam allowances. Stitch a triangular unit to each side of framed quilt block; resulting square should measure 9¾″ inside seam allowances. Make two strips G-F-E-F-G as shown in piecing diagram. Set aside. Stitch remaining E's to either side of square, then stitch an embroidered border to outside edges of E's.

Make corner blocks: stitch an I to each side of H patches to form a square, 2½″ inside seam allowances. Adhering to planned arrangement, make two strips joining corner blocks to remaining G's and embroidered borders; stitch these strips to G-F-E-F-G strips. Stitch resulting units to top and bottom of quilt, taking care to match seams. Quilt top should measure 13½″ square inside seam allowances.

Assembly and Binding: Cut backing and batting 1½″ larger all around. Assemble layers, with patchwork centered right side up on top. From blue print, cut binding, adding seam allowance: two 3″ × 13½″, two 3″ × 16½″. Pin shorter lengths to top and bottom of quilt top; stitch through all layers. In same manner, sew longer lengths to sides. Press outside edges of strips ½″ to wrong side. turn binding over edges of batting and backing and pin to backing, mitering corners. Slip-stitch in place.

Quilting (optional): Hand-quilt in the seams around framed quilt block and either side of E and F pieces.

COLOR AND STITCH KEY

FRENCH KNOTS

Ⓐ Light Lavender #108
Ⓧ Medium Citrus #301

LONG STRAIGHT STITCH

Medium Citrus #301

BACKSTITCH

— — — Apricot #323
═══ Medium China Rose #50
·········· Dark China Rose #54
——— Dark Spruce #211
▬▬▬ Medium Coffee #358
▬ ▬ Medium Cobalt Blue #130

CROSS-STITCH

- Pale Salmon #6
- Light Salmon #8
- Light China Rose #48
- Medium China Rose #50
- Light Lavender #108
- Light Cobalt Blue #128
- Light Mint Green #203
- Medium Spruce #209
- Light Yellow #292
- Light Citrus #300
- Medium Citrus #301
- Medium Coffee #358
- Light Ecru #386
- Sand Stone #886
- Medium Wheat #943

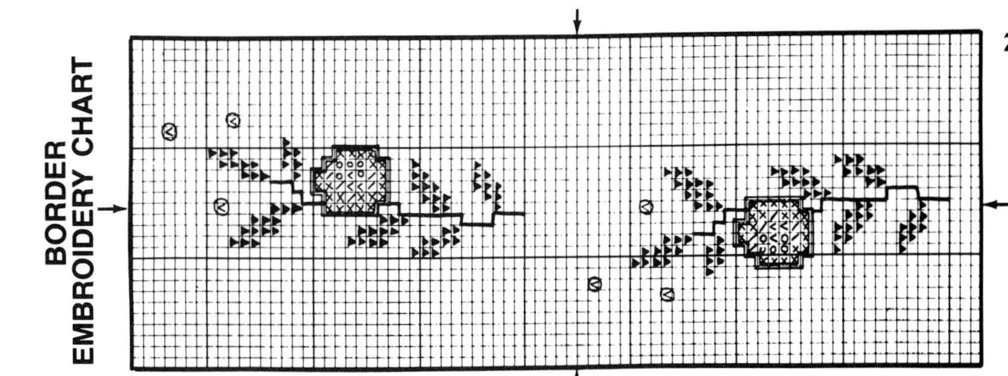
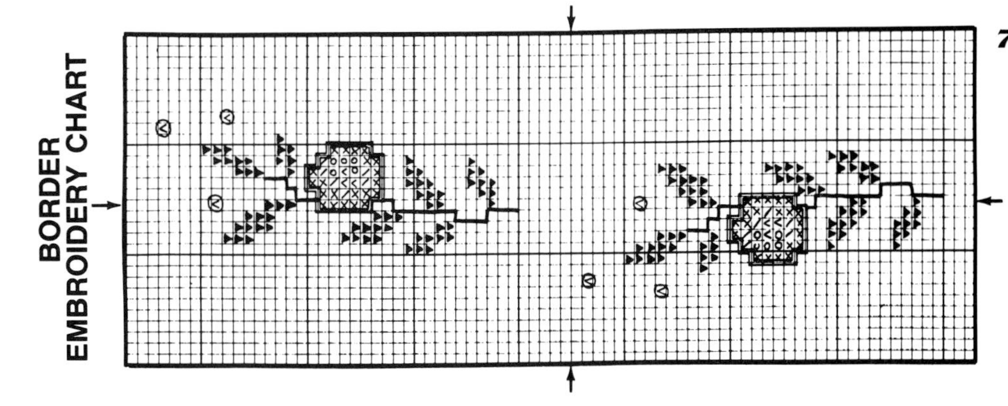

BORDER EMBROIDERY CHART

CENTER BLOCK—CHART 1

CENTER EMBROIDERY BLOCK—CHART 2

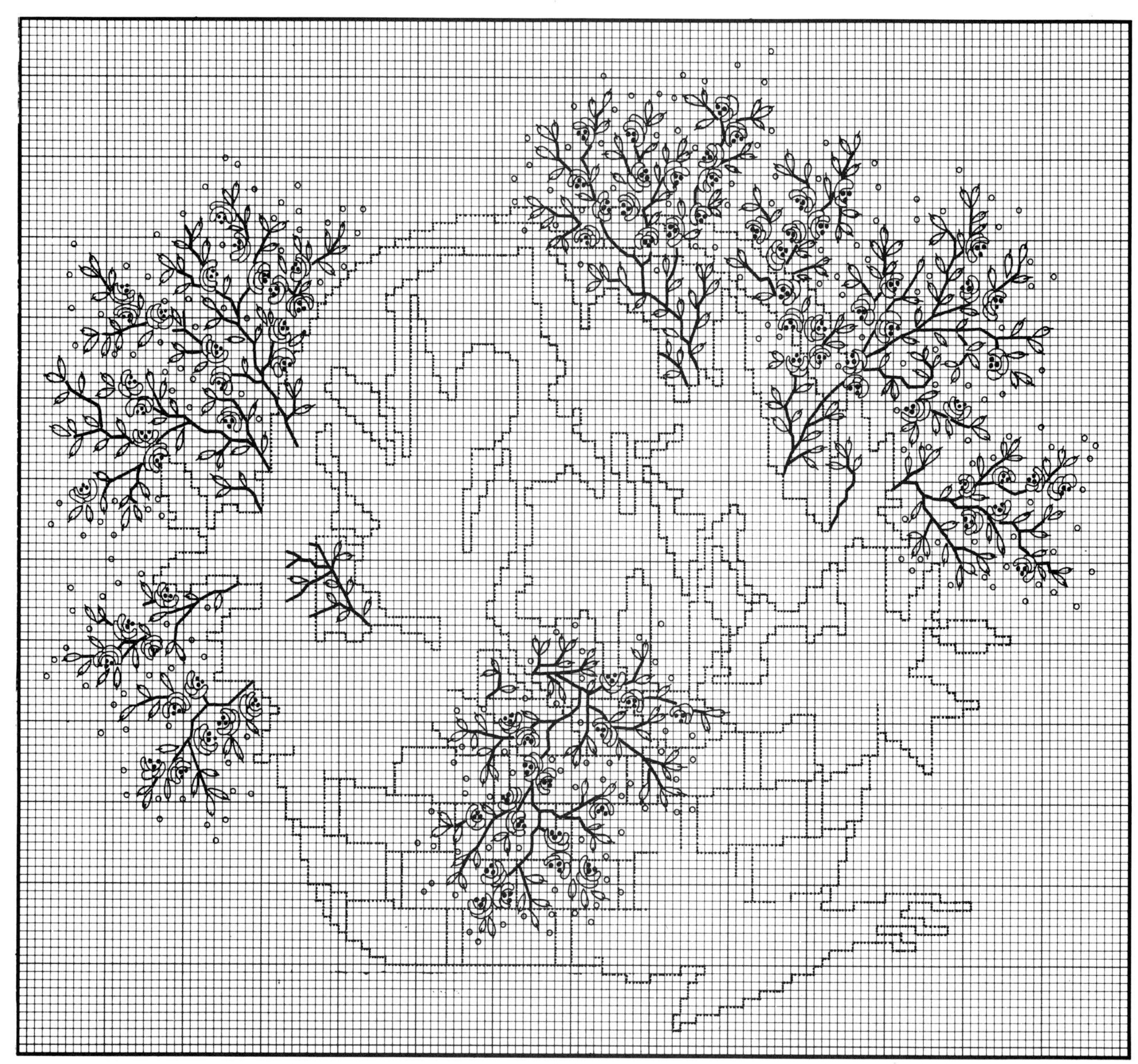

COLOR AND STITCH KEY

··········	Outline of Chart 1 Design
——	Backstitches in Dark Spruce #211
∴	French Knots in Pale Salmon #6
o	French Knot in Medium Cobalt Blue #138
(leaf)	Lazy Daisy Stitch in Dark Spruce #211
(arc)	Bullion Stitch in Medium Cobalt Blue #130

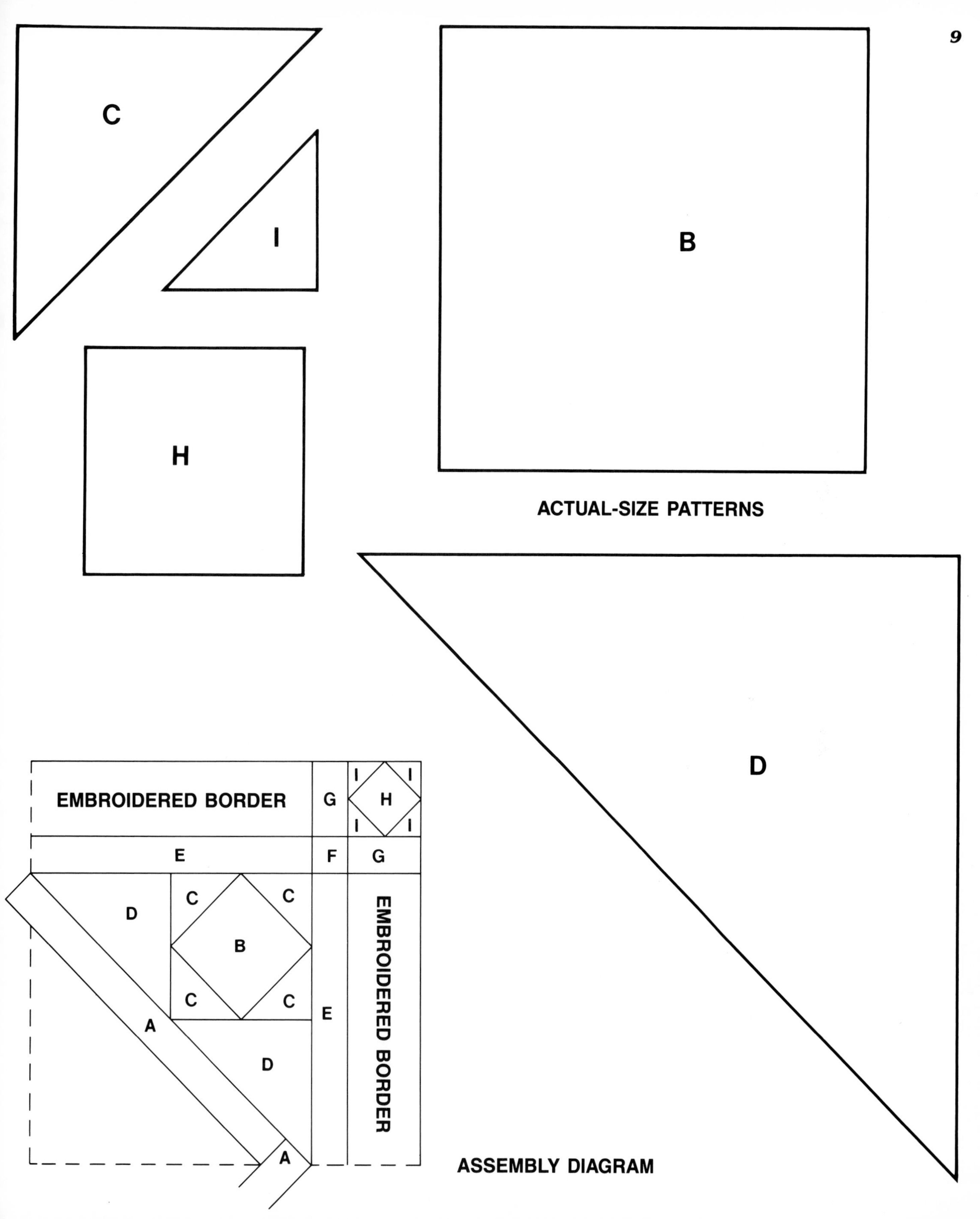

ACTUAL-SIZE PATTERNS

ASSEMBLY DIAGRAM

Gazebo in a Flowering Garden with Reflecting Pond

Flower-filled garden is "painted" in cross-stitch; metallic filaments give the pond a special sheen.

Garden Gazebo Picture

SIZE:
Approximately 7¾″ × 9¾″.

EQUIPMENT:
Sewing needle. Basting thread. Straight pin. Embroidery hoop or frame (optional). Fine tapestry needle. Embroidery scissors. Magnetic stitch finder (optional—to aid in reading chart). Iron.

MATERIALS:
White 14-count Aida fabric piece 16″ × 18″. Susan Bates Anchor® six-strand embroidery floss, one skein each color listed in color key, except two skeins each light sapphire #158 and light avocado #266. Balger® metallic blending filament, one 50-meter reel each sky blue #014, pearl #032, and peacock #085; to order from The Daisy Chain, see Buyers' Guide, page 174.

DIRECTIONS:
Read Cross-Stitch How-To's, page 177. To prevent fabric from raveling, overcast all raw edges. Lay piece on work surface with shorter edges at sides. From upper right corner, measure 4″ down and 8½″ to the left; mark with a pin for first stitch.

Work design in cross-stitch, following chart and beginning at pin with stitch indicated by arrow. Each square on chart represents one "square" of fabric threads. Different symbols represent different colors. Solid lines are used in two ways: to separate color areas on chart and to indicate backstitching around gazebo, to be worked after cross-stitching is completed.

Separate strands of floss and work all stitches with two strands in tapestry needle. As you work, fill in all blank areas of chart so that design is solidly stitched. Referring to color photograph, work the blank areas as follows: Sky, light sapphire; trees and lawn, light avocado; pond, medium denim blue, and gazebo reflection, white; large violet, rose, and pink bushes, light avocado; red bushes, light burgundy or light avocado, whichever is not symboled (e.g., if medium burgundy and light avocado are symboled, the blank areas are to be worked in light burgundy); small violet bush at base of tree, light violet; three red bushes in background, light avocado. For pond, work with two strands floss and one strand blending filament where indicated by symbols used. When working with blending filament, knot the filament onto the needle as follows: Cut filament 21″ long; form a loop 3″ from end of strand and thread loop through eye of needle. Pull loop over point of needle, then pull on filament ends to tighten loop around end of eye. Add floss.

When all cross-stitching is completed, work backstitches to outline gazebo as indicated, using two strands dark gray floss (see stitch details, page 178). Press completed work gently on a padded surface. Mount and frame as desired.

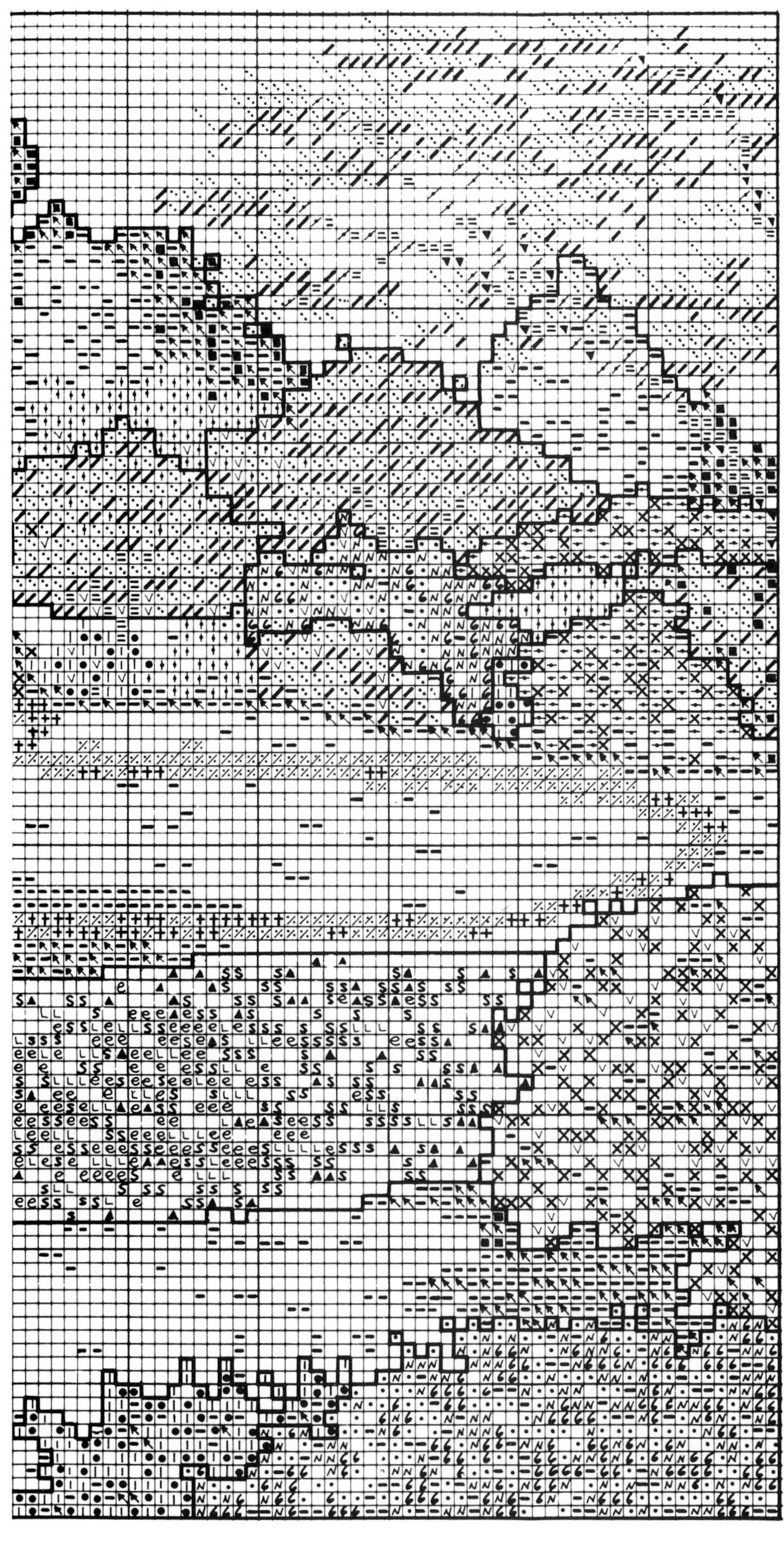

GARDEN GAZEBO

- Light Sapphire #158 (2)
- Light Avocado #266 (2)
- Medium Avocado #267
- Dark Avocado #268 *
- Deep Avocado #269
- Light Burgundy #19
- Medium Burgundy #20
- Light Carnation #27
- Medium Carnation #28
- Dark Carnation #29
- Light Antique Rose #73
- Medium Antique Rose #75
- Light Violet #96
- Medium Violet #98
- Light Tawny #898
- Medium Tawny #903
- Dark Tawny #905
- Light Desert #372
- Medium Desert #373
- White #2
- Light Gray #397
- Medium Gray #398
- Dark Gray #401 (backstitching)
- L [Light Blue Mist #847 / Pearl filament #032
- e [Medium Blue Mist #848 / Sky Blue filament #014
- S [Light Denim Blue #920 / Sky Blue filament #014
- Medium Denim Blue #921
- [Dark Avocado #268 * / Peacock filament #085

* Buy one skein Dark Avocado #268, even though it is listed in color key twice.

Place Mats as Fresh as Spring

Oval place mats bring springtime crocus and chirping robins into your home.

Place Mats

SIZES:

Each mat, approximately 17″ in diameter.

EQUIPMENT:

Ruler. Scissors. Pencil. Embroidery hoop. Tapestry and sewing needles. Straight pins. Masking tape.

MATERIALS:

Off-white 22-count linen, 20″ square for each. DMC six-strand embroidery floss, one skein of each color in color keys. Sewing thread to match fabric.

DIRECTIONS:

Tape fabric edges to prevent raveling. Find center of each design area by folding square in half horizontally and vertically; mark center with straight pin.

Read Cross-Stitch How-To's, page 177. Each mat is worked entirely in cross-stitch. Each square on quarter-charts represents two threads horizontally and two threads vertically. To begin embroidery, find center square on charts (center rows marked by arrows). Following charts and color keys, embroider designs. Use two strands of floss in needle unless otherwise noted in parentheses within color keys. Do not make knots. Begin by leaving 1″ of floss end on fabric back and working over it to secure; to end, run strand through stitches on back. When embroidery is finished, block following directions in Embroidery Basics, page 175.

To finish each mat, count 25 threads out from outside edge of border stitches and mark with pins. Cut off excess fabric at pin line; count five threads in from fabric edge and fold fabric under, then fold fabric under again the same amount. Pin folded edge in place, then hem from back of fabric, using small, invisible stitches.

ROBIN ON A HOLLY SPRIG

- Dark Green #3345 (4)
- Dark Medium Green #3346 (4)
- Medium Green #470
- Light Green #471 (5)
- Dark Brown #838 (4)
- Medium Gray-Brown #610
- Light Gray-Brown #611
- Black #310
- Medium Gray #414
- Light Gray #3024
- Burnt Orange #921
- Light Orange #922 (3)
- Red #349 (5)
- Yellow-Green #472

ROBIN AND HOLLY

GARLAND OF CROCUS

- Λ Dark Lilac #552
- ☒ Dark Medium Lilac #553
- ◪ Medium Lilac #554
- · Light Lilac #211
- ● Dark Faded Green #937
- ‖ Dark Green #986
- V Medium Green#320
- ∴ Light Green #3348
- ◉ Orange #741

Wreath of Roses Tablecloth

Elegant roses, cross-stitched over penelope canvas, ring the center of a purchased tablecloth.

Roses Tablecloth

SIZE:

Embroidered area is approximately 19″ in diameter. Although shown on a round table, embroidery would be equally as effective on a square or rectangle.

EQUIPMENT:

Embroidery and sewing needles. Scissors. Pencil. Ruler. Basting thread. Tweezers. Straight pins.

MATERIALS:

Ready-made linen or linen-like cloth with smooth finish in size desired. Penelope (cross-stitch) canvas, 10 mesh-to-the-inch, about 22″ square. DMC six-strand embroidery floss, one skein of each color listed in color key, unless otherwise indicated in parentheses.

DIRECTIONS:

Center of fabric must be determined before beginning embroidery. To find center, fold cloth horizontally and vertically into quarters and mark center point with a pin. Find center of penelope canvas; lightly mark center mesh with pencil. Matching center points, place penelope canvas on top of tablecloth. Pin and baste canvas in place.

Center of cloth is indicated by X at center of chart, shown in quarters on the following pages. Counting off one mesh of canvas for every square on chart, determine your own starting point for embroidering design.

Read Cross-Stitch How-To's, page 177, paying special attention to "On Penelope Canvas." Using four strands of floss in needle, cross-stitch entire design. Each stitch is made over one mesh of canvas. (*Note:* To make chart easier to read, large areas of the same color are marked off and designated by number; these numbers appear in the color key.)

If desired, single roses may be scattered on overhang. Additional floss and canvas will be needed. To determine placement of single motifs, lightly mark off diameter of table in center of cloth. About ½″ below marked line, evenly space desired number of 6″ squares of penelope canvas. Repeat a second row of penelope squares directly below first approximately 1″ up from hemline. Center squares of penelope canvas between top and bottom rows for middle row. Baste all squares in place, embroider following single rose chart.

When embroidery is complete, remove threads from penelope canvas as directed in Cross-Stitch How-To's. Steam-press if necessary.

UPPER LEFT QUARTER

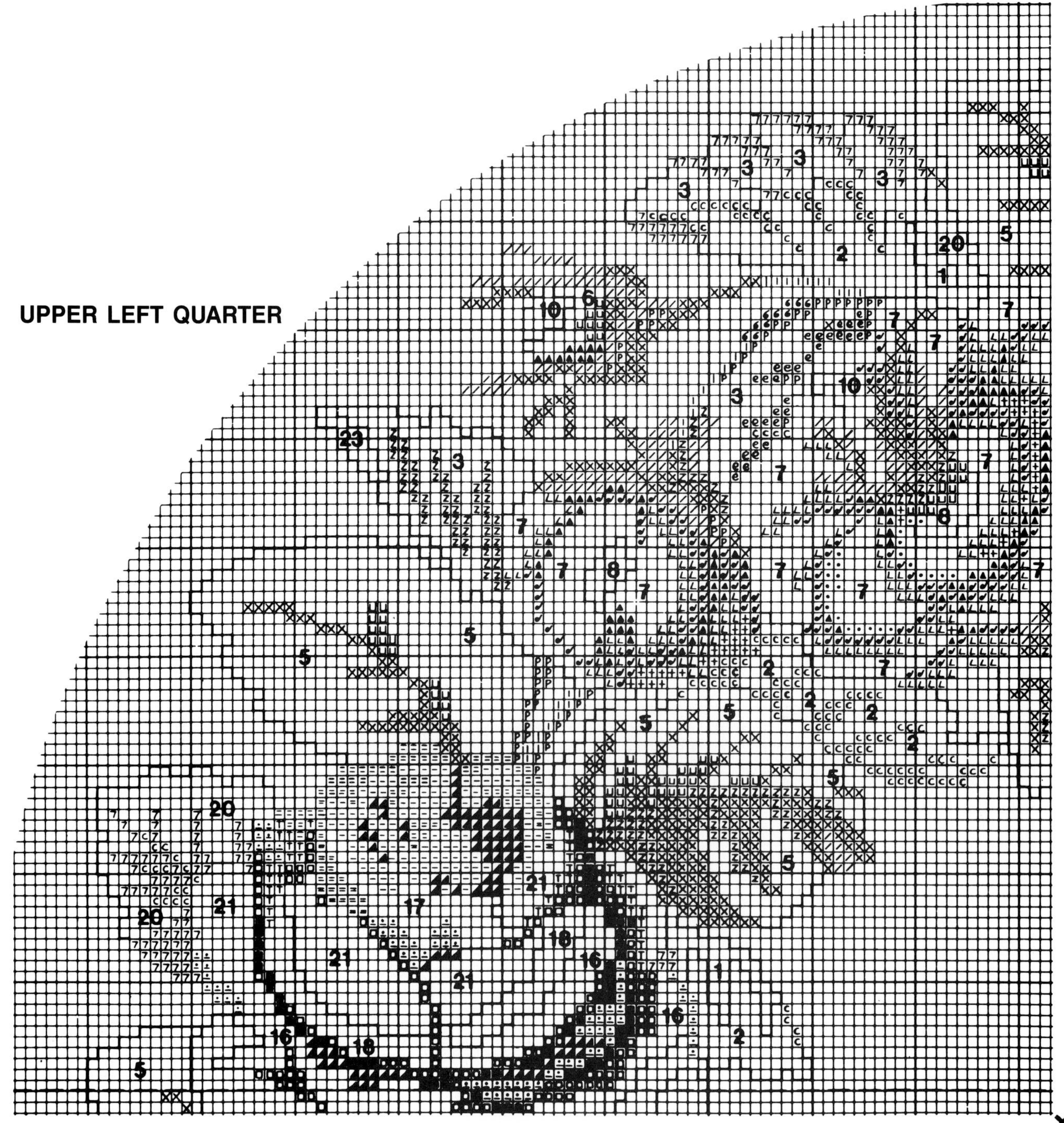

COLOR KEY

- 1 Deep Green #367
- 2 Medium Green #320
- 3 Light Green #368
- 20 Pale Green #369
- 23 Deep Olive #937
- 4 Medium Olive #469
- 5 Light Olive #470 (3)
- Pale Olive #471
- Medium Yellow-Green #732
- Light Yellow-Green #734
- Pale Yellow-Green #472
- 7 Medium Peach #353 (2)
- 8 Pale Peach #754
- 10 Rosy Peach #351
- Deep Rose #326
- 13 Medium Rose #309
- 14 Light Rose #899
- 15 Deep Pink #326
- 16 Light Pink #776
- 17 Pale Pink #818
- 18 Ice Pink #819
- 6 Cinnamon Red #347 (2)
- Deep Garnet #814
- 9 Medium Garnet #815 (2)
- 11 Flag Red #304 (2)
- Watermelon #891
- Taupe #223
- Toast #760
- 12 Mahogany #902
- 25 Deep Gold #782
- Medium Gold #783
- 22 Light Gold #725
- 19 Yellow #726
- 24 Gray #646
- 21 White (2)

UPPER RIGHT QUARTER

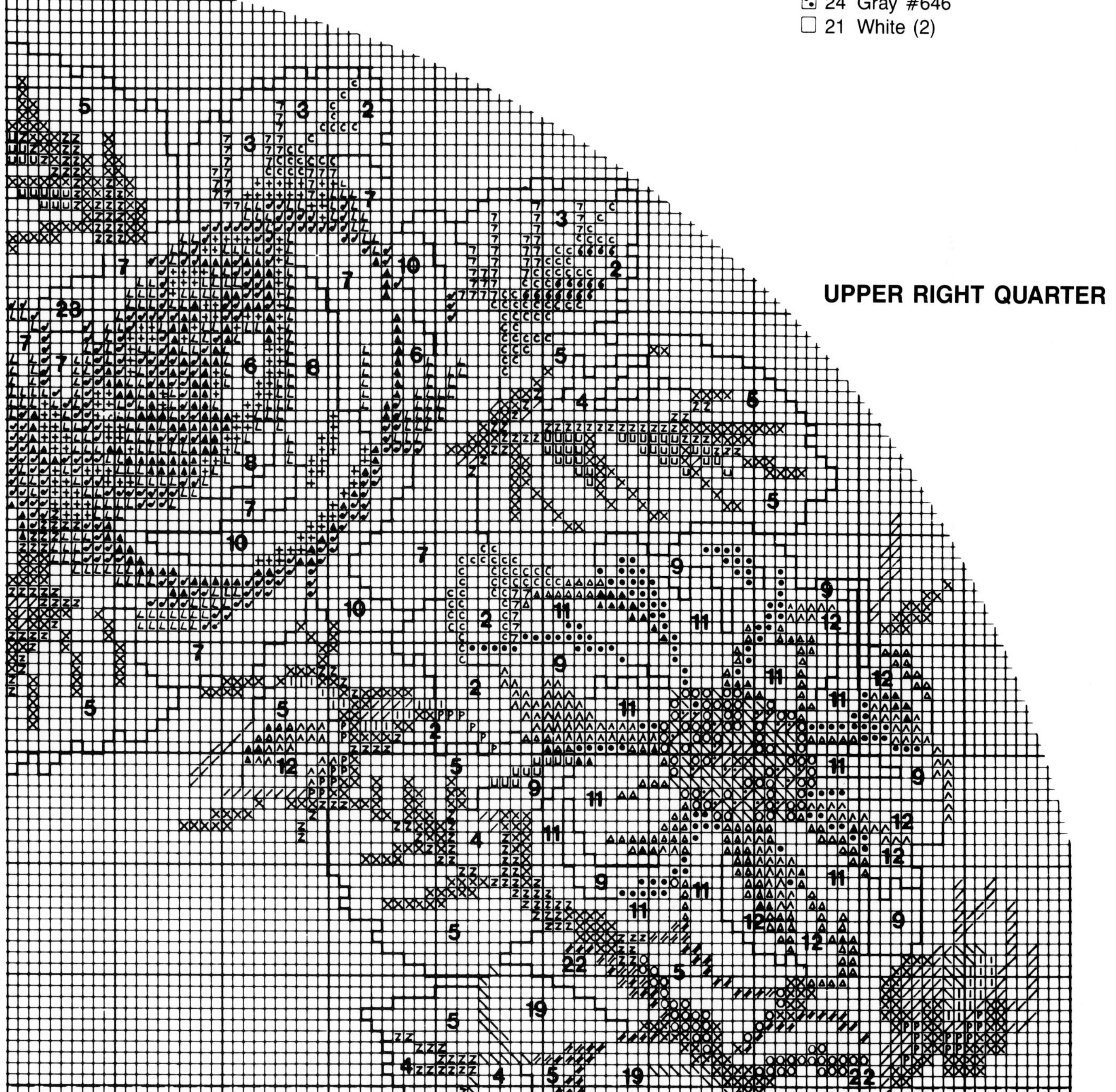

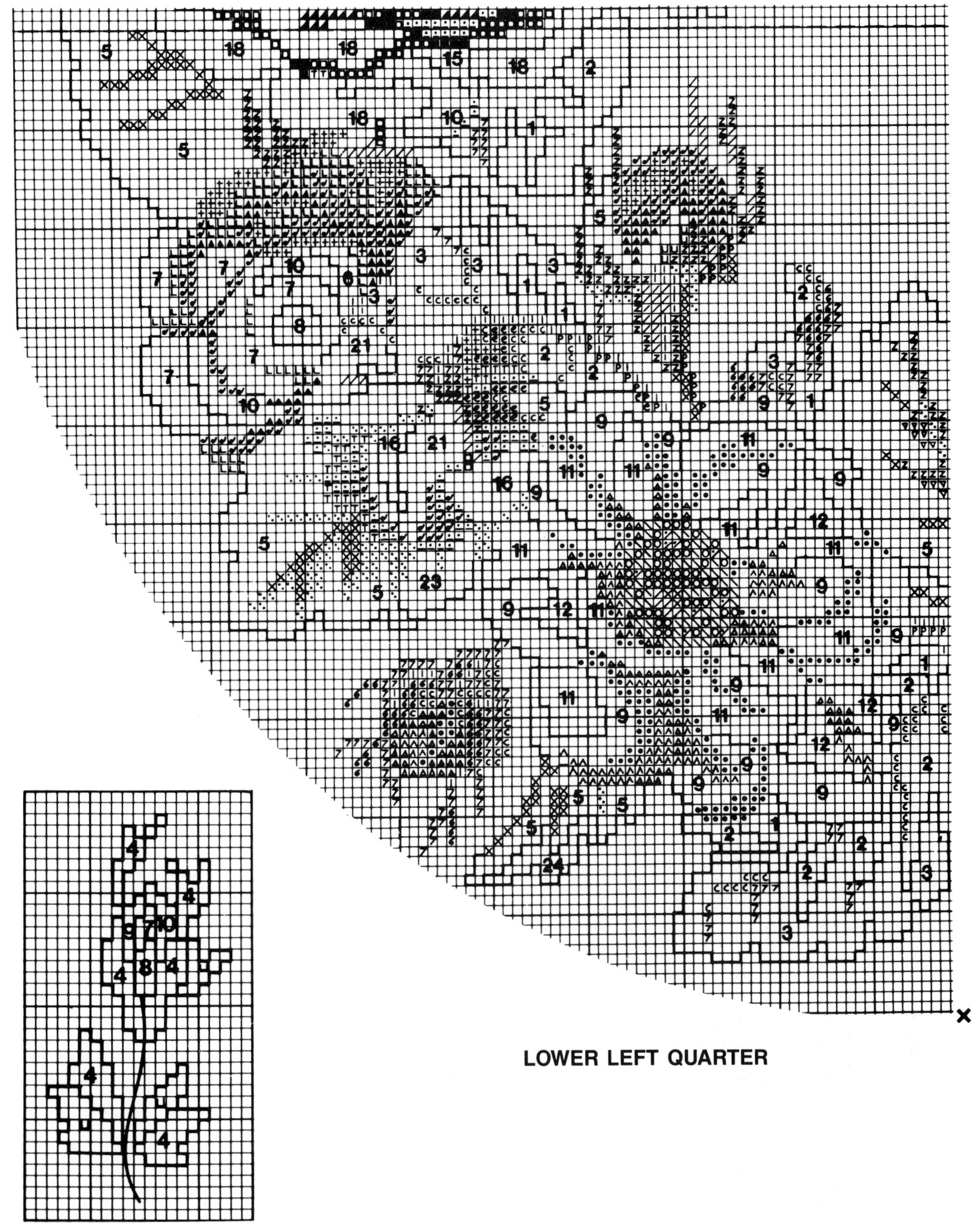

LOWER LEFT QUARTER

SINGLE ROSE

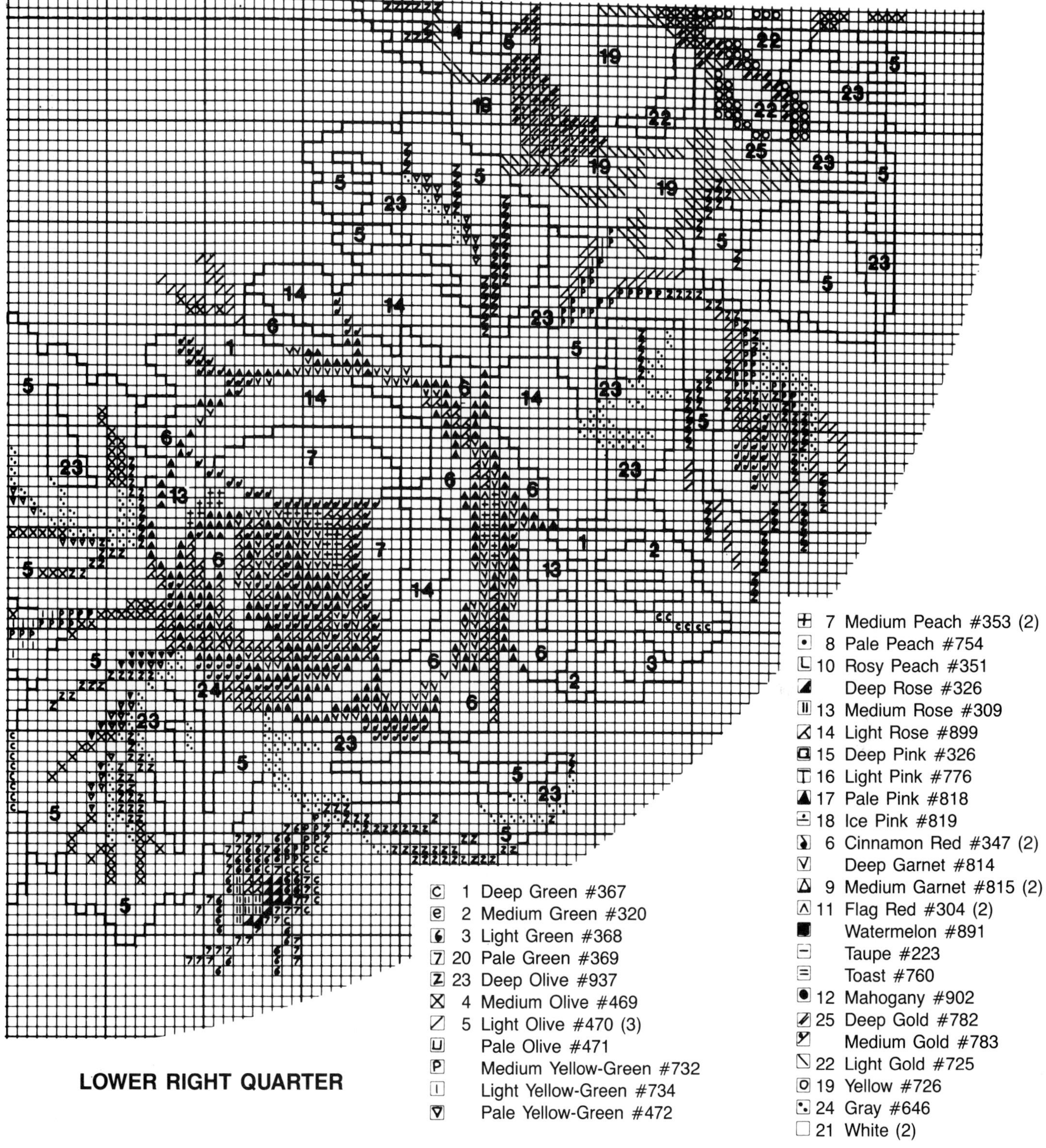

LOWER RIGHT QUARTER

- 1 Deep Green #367
- 2 Medium Green #320
- 3 Light Green #368
- 20 Pale Green #369
- 23 Deep Olive #937
- 4 Medium Olive #469
- 5 Light Olive #470 (3)
- Pale Olive #471
- Medium Yellow-Green #732
- Light Yellow-Green #734
- Pale Yellow-Green #472

- 7 Medium Peach #353 (2)
- 8 Pale Peach #754
- 10 Rosy Peach #351
- Deep Rose #326
- 13 Medium Rose #309
- 14 Light Rose #899
- 15 Deep Pink #326
- 16 Light Pink #776
- 17 Pale Pink #818
- 18 Ice Pink #819
- 6 Cinnamon Red #347 (2)
- Deep Garnet #814
- 9 Medium Garnet #815 (2)
- 11 Flag Red #304 (2)
- Watermelon #891
- Taupe #223
- Toast #760
- 12 Mahogany #902
- 25 Deep Gold #782
- Medium Gold #783
- 22 Light Gold #725
- 19 Yellow #726
- 24 Gray #646
- 21 White (2)

Tulip Time Trio

Tulips stitched on linen enhance a pillow, mirror frame, and box lid.

Mirror, Pillow and Box Cover

SIZES:

Mirror, 9¾" × 13¾"; pillow, 12½" × 11¾"; box, 5" diameter.

EQUIPMENT:

Tape measure. Ruler. Straight pins. Scissors. Pencil. Masking tape. Tapestry and sewing needles. Embroidery hoop (optional). Paintbrush for box. Compass. Steam iron. Tailor's chalk.

MATERIALS:

White or off-white 22-count linen fabric 36" wide, ⅝ yard (enough fabric for all three items). Matching sewing thread. DMC six-strand embroidery floss in colors listed in color key, one skein of each for mirror and lid cover and two skeins of each for pillow. All-purpose glue. **For Mirror:** Mirror, 9¾" × 13¾"; heavy buckram, 9¾" × 19¾"; corrugated cardboard, 9" × 13"; picture hanging wire; narrow velvet ribbon, 1¼ yards; small beads in same colors as tulips, 28. **For Pillow:** Cotton fabric for back in desired color, 13½" × 12¾"; muslin, two 14½" × 13¾" pieces; polyester fiberfill for stuffing. **For Box:** Round wooden box with lid, 5" diameter; acrylic paint in color desired; one small glass button; ball fringe to match linen with ¾" pompons, 15¾".

GENERAL DIRECTIONS:

Read Cross-Stitch How-To's, page 177. Cut linen to size given in individual directions below. Tape edges to prevent raveling.

Complete charts are given for mirror and lid cover; quarter-chart is given for pillow. Find center of linen as directed in individual directions; mark with pin. Place fabric tautly and evenly in hoop with pin in center.

Thread embroidery needle with three strands of the six-strand floss. Follow color key and chart for design; begin embroidery at center. Each square of chart represents two threads horizontally and two threads vertically. Work crosses over two threads with all underneath stitches going in one direction and all top stitches going in opposite direction.

(continued)

MIRROR

Cut linen $11\frac{1}{4}'' \times 20\frac{3}{4}''$. Place linen flat on table, wrong side up. Place mirror in center of linen, with longer edges of mirror and linen parallel; fold extended sides of linen over mirror. Indicate side edges of mirror on linen by creasing along folds and marking lightly with tailor's chalk on right side. Remove mirror and turn linen to right side. Mark a line ½″ from each end, parallel to first lines. Using long running stitches, baste along the four lines, thus marking off the two side panels to be embroidered. Embroider mirror's left-side panel first, which is now at your right. Fold and crease fabric in half lengthwise to indicate horizontal center line; mark center point on the line 1½″ from vertical line at far right. Begin working design at center point, indicated on chart by arrow. Sew a bead above each tulip, as indicated on chart by black squares. To embroider remaining panel, work design in reverse.

After steam-pressing linen, center buckram on wrong side; pin in place. At sides, fold ½″ linen margins over buckram; press. With right sides facing, fold each side of fabric along inner basted line. Press. Stitch top and bottom edges of pockets with ¾″ seams. Turn to right side; remove basting; press. At center areas of top and bottom, fold margins over buckram and press. Slip mirror into frame.

To hang mirror, mark vertical center of flat surface of cardboard (make sure long edges of cardboard are at top and bottom). Mark a point at each side 5″ from center and 1″ above center. Make holes at each point. Cut long length of wire; insert wire end in one hole; twist wire to secure, then tape over the hole. Repeat with other end at other hole, pulling wire through holes to adjust length of hang. Glue cardboard to mirror back and let glue dry thoroughly. Hang mirror. Glue velvet ribbon over wire to cover. Make velvet bow and glue to cover point of hanging. Cut two lengths of velvet ribbon and glue along exposed mirror edges at top and bottom.

PILLOW

Cut linen fabric $13\frac{1}{2}'' \times 12\frac{3}{4}''$. Find center of fabric by folding in half horizontally and then vertically. Turn so that longer edges are vertical. Larger area of chart, marked off by dash lines, indicates one-quarter of entire design. Work this quarter in upper left corner, starting from center of fabric (indicated on chart by intersection of dash lines).

Repeat three times to complete entire design. Additional vertical and horizontal rows (marked by dashes) are given to indicate beginning of repeat pattern.

Pin steam-pressed embroidered linen to cotton fabric, right sides together. Stitch all around with ½″ seams, leaving 10½″ open along one side. Turn to right side.

To make inner pillow, sew muslin rectangles together with ½″ seams, leaving 6″ opening along one side. Turn to right side and stuff fully. Turn raw edges in and slip-stitch closed.

Insert inner pillow in pillow cover. Turn raw edges in; slip-stitch closed.

(continued)

BOX COVER

Paint box with acrylic paint in desired color.

While box is drying, cut linen 8¾″ square. Find the center of linen in the same manner as for pillow. Work center and embroider outward following color key. Sew button to motif center.

With a pencil and compass, mark a 7¼″-diameter circle around embroidery. Cut out circle. Turn edge under ¼″, steam press. Make long running stitch ⅛″ from edge of circle; place linen over lid and pull running stitch thread to gather. Ease fabric puckers evenly around lid; knot thread to secure. Glue edge of linen to lid, then glue ball fringe around linen edges.

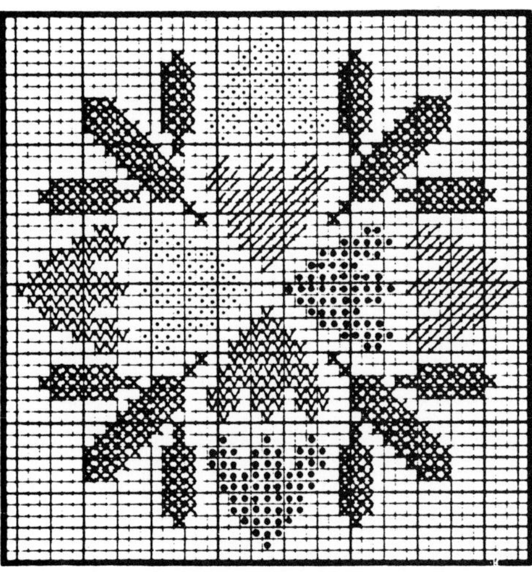

BOX

TULIP TIME TRIO

- ⊠ Pale Green #912
- ◙ Dark Rose #326
- ⊡ Medium Rose #961
- ⧄ Blue #797
- ☑ Lilac #208

MIRROR

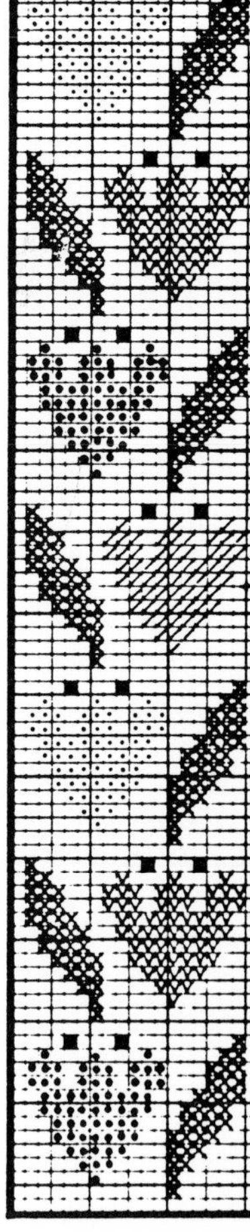

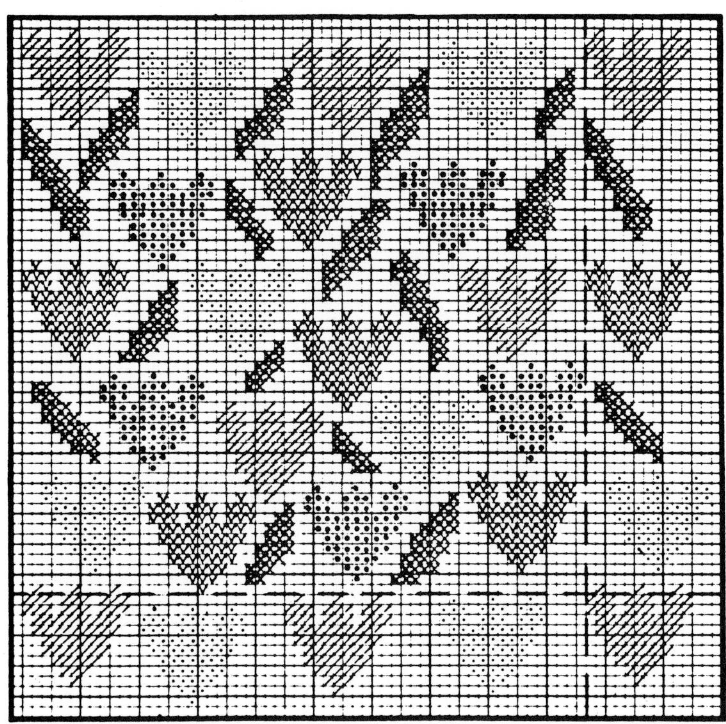

PILLOW

Violet Trellis Basket

Delicate violets repeat around a basket that's perfect for displaying a nosegay of cut flowers.

Basket

SIZE:

9¼″ × 6¼″ × 6¼″ high, plus handle.

EQUIPMENT:

Pencil. Ruler. Tape measure. Masking tape. Scissors. Mat knife. Straight pins. Tapestry and sewing needles. Embroidery hoop. Iron.

MATERIALS:

Zweigart® 27-count "Linda" fabric 32½″ wide, ½ yard light blue; to order from Hansi's Haus, see Buyers' Guide, page 174. Yellow cotton fabric 36″ wide, ½ yard. Six-strand embroidery floss: blue, 6 skeins; green, 4 skeins; yellow, 2 skeins. Sewing thread: light blue and contrasting color. Iron-on fusible webbing, piece 18″ × 1¼″. Self-Stick Needlework Mounting Board, one sheet 16″ × 20″. Medium-weight cardboard, piece 18″ × 1¼″. White craft glue.

DIRECTIONS:

On mounting board, mark five rectangles: two 9¼″ × 6¼″, two 6¼″ square, one 4″ × 6¾″. On the first two, draw lines from bottom edge to top corners as shown in diagram; using mat knife, cut on lines (discarding shaded areas) for front and back of basket. Do not remove protective backing from board. On the second two rectangles, draw lines to top corners in same manner as before but measuring in 1⅛″ from bottom corners; cut out for sides of basket. Cut out fifth rectangle for bottom of basket.

From one selvage edge of Linda cloth, cut strip 3″ × 18″ for handle; set aside. Using the five mounting board pieces as patterns, place them on wrong side of remaining Linda cloth, at least 1″ apart and 1″ in from edges

(continued)

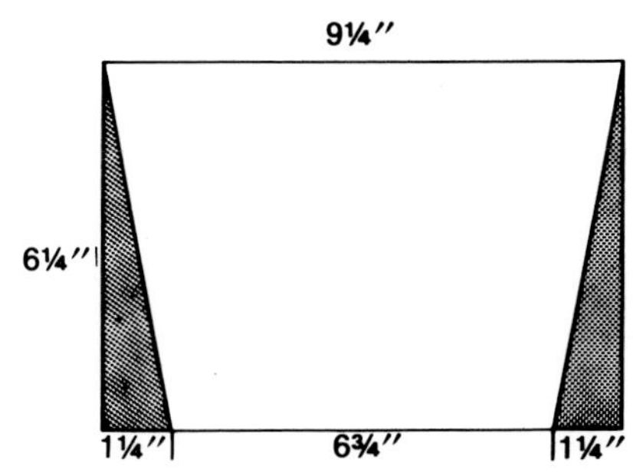

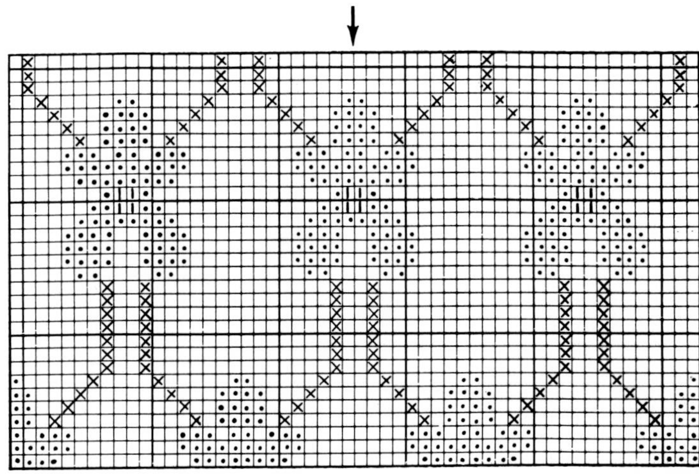

of fabric, and with parallel edges on grain of fabric. Draw around pieces with sharp pencil held at an outward angle. Set pieces aside. With contrasting thread, baste along marked lines, being sure that thread follows straight grain of fabric on all parallel lines. Do not cut out fabric pieces. Turn fabric to right side for embroidery.

Embroidery: Read Cross-Stitch How-To's, page 177. Tape edges of fabric to prevent raveling. Work design in cross-stitch, following chart and color key. Separate the six strands of floss and work with two strands in embroidery needle throughout. Find center of top edge of front piece, indicated on chart by arrow; measure down ¼″ and mark with straight pin for top of center flower. Insert fabric in hoop to keep it taut, centering front piece within. Beginning with first blue stitch to right or left of straight pin, work design from top center out to right and to left and downward, repeating design to fill marked area. Remove hoop and reposition over back piece; work design as for front. Embroider sides in same manner or leave blank, as desired. Leave bottom piece blank. When all embroidery is completed, steam-press gently on padded surface.

Cut out all five pieces ½″ beyond basting. Cut a lining piece from yellow fabric same size as each blue piece.

Assembling: Read manufacturer's directions for mounting board. Attach each blue piece to corresponding mounting piece, as follows: Place blue piece wrong side up on flat work surface. Remove protective sheet from board. Centering board over blue piece, adhesive side down, firmly press board onto fabric, matching board edges with basted outlines. Turn both pieces over, so that board is underneath; smooth fabric tautly over board; press firmly in place to adhere. Fold raw edges over board to wrong side; glue to secure. Carefully remove basting.

Right sides facing out, pin the four embroidered pieces together along slanting edges to form four-sided basket. Slip-stitch adjoining edges with matching thread. Place basket bottom on work surface with board face up. Place basket on top, narrow end down and matching edges; pin in place; slip-stitch together.

Handle: Press long edges of handle piece ¼″ to wrong side; place wrong side up on work surface. Place fusible webbing on cardboard strip, matching edges; center both lengthwise on handle piece. Fold long edges of fabric over webbing, until they meet; press with iron to secure.

Lining: Press raw edges of each lining piece ½″ to wrong side. Glue each piece to corresponding basket part with wrong sides facing and edges even.

Purple Iris Triptych

Freestanding triptych of colorful irises is stitched on perforated paper.

Triptych

SIZE:

Screen, approximately 9″ × 23″.

EQUIPMENT:

Pencil. Ruler. Scissors. Tapestry needle. Drill. Screwdriver. Staple gun or tack hammer. Mat knife and metal straight edge (optional).

MATERIALS:

Ecru 14-count perforated paper: one 8″ × 10″ sheet and two 5″ × 7″ sheets. DMC six-strand embroidery floss: one skein each red-violet #552, blue-violet #333, light blue #799, and dark blue #797; two skeins each light green #907 and dark green #3345. Three matching wooden frames: one 8″ × 10″ and two 5″ × 7″. Two pieces of plate glass to fit each frame. Two pairs (four) ¾″-long brass hinges with screws. Staples or ½″ brads. Ecru mat board (optional).

DIRECTIONS:

Measure and mark starting points on perforated paper as follows: Right Panel: measure 1″ down and 1½″ from upper left corner of a 5″ × 7″ sheet. Center Panel: measure ⅜″ down and 4¾″ in from upper right corner of 8″ × 10″ sheet. Left Panel: measure 1⅜″ down and 1⅞″ in from upper right corner of a 5″ × 7″ sheet. Read Cross-Stitch How-To's, page 177. Following full-color charts, stitch motifs with three strands floss in needle, beginning each sheet with stitch marked by arrow on chart. Make wrong side of work as neat as possible: Do not carry floss across back of work as it will show; weave ends into wrong side and trim floss ends closely.

When embroidery is completed, arrange frames in order on a flat surface, wrong side up. Placing hinge pivots toward front and hinges 1¼″ from top and bottom of side frames, mark positions of hinge holes on all frames. Drill holes at markings; do not attach hinges until directed.

Clean glass pieces thoroughly; place one piece into each frame. Add embroidery, right side down, then remaining glass. If the frame is deep, insert ¼″-wide strips of mat board into frame and over the glass edges to reduce the amount of play. Secure glass (and cardboard) in frames with staples or brads. Attach hinges to assemble screen as shown. Clean outer glass surfaces.

PURPLE IRIS TRIPTYCH
Red-Violet #552
Blue-Violet #333
Light Blue #799
Dark Blue #797
Light Green #907
Dark Green #3345

Garden Potpourri Lids and Sachets

The sweet aroma of garden potpourri is enhanced by floral motifs on sachets and jar lids.

Sachets and Glass Lids

SIZES:

Sachets, 3½″ square; lids, 2¾″ in diameter or size to fit glasses of your choice.

EQUIPMENT:

Pencil. Ruler. Scissors. Tapestry and sewing needles. Small embroidery hoop. Straight pin. Sewing machine. Iron. For lids, compass.

MATERIALS:

White Zweigart® 25-count "Dublin" linen, 55″ wide (to order from Hansi's Haus, see Buyers' Guide, page 174): For each sachet: two 4″ squares (cut out after embroidering); for each lid: one circle of fabric, diameter of glass plus 1″ all around (cut out after embroidering). DMC six-strand embroidery floss, one skein of each color to be used (see color photograph and color key): purple #553, red #321, blue-green #991, light green #966, yellow #726, turquoise #806, lime green #581, pink #957, blue #799, olive #580, orange #350, peach #352, gold #922, fuchsia #601. **For each sachet:** Satin ribbon ¼″ wide, 24″ long, color to match cross-stitch design. Thread: white, and color to match ribbon. Potpourri, about ¼ cup. **For each glass lid:** Mat board. Small amount of batting. Satin cord, long enough to fit around top of glass plus 2½″. White craft glue.

DIRECTIONS:

With pencil, mark cutting lines on linen: for sachet front, a 4″ square with sides along grain of fabric; for glass lid, a circle measuring 1″ more all around than diameter of rim of glass (use compass). Fold square or circle in quarters to determine center; mark with a straight pin. Insert fabric in embroidery hoop to keep it taut. Squares on charts represent threads on fabric; symbols represent different colors.

Read Cross-Stitch How-To's, page 177. Starting at center of design (use arrows on chart to find center) and at pin, embroider designs in cross-stitch. Follow charts and color photograph or color key.

Assembly: Sachet: Cut out square for sachet front plus a square, same size, for the sachet back: cutting lines should follow grain of fabric. Place sachet front and back together with right sides facing. Machine-stitch around three sides and corners of fourth side, ¼″ from edges. Clip corners; turn sachet right side out. Fold in edge of fourth side ¼″; press sachet. Insert potpourri, then slip-stitch fourth side closed. Machine-stitch around all four sides of sachet, ½″ from seams. Beginning at top center of cross-stitch design and leaving a tail of 6″, slip-stitch satin ribbon around sachet front, covering machine stitching; miter-fold at corners. Tie ends of ribbon in a bow. **Glass lids:** Place glass upside down on a sheet of paper; trace around rim of glass. Use compass to draw a circle inside of tracing, with a diameter ¼″ smaller than traced circle. Use compass to draw two circles on mat board, one same size as smaller circle drawn, another ¼″ larger in diameter than traced circle. Cut out the smaller paper circle and two mat board circles. Dot top surface of large mat-board circle with glue, then place on it a layer of batting, cut to fit. Press cross-stitch lightly and center over batting. Fold edges of linen to back of board,

(continued)

glue down, and glue paper circle to the center of the back, hiding all raw edges. Place lid under the weight of a book until glue sets. Glue small mat-board circle directly over paper circle. When glue has dried, tie satin cord around rim of smaller mat-board circle; knot ends.

COLOR KEY

- ● Blue-Green
- ☒ Blue
- O Orange
- Y Yellow
- ⁄ Turquoise
- ╲ Lime Green
- · Peach
- + Gold
- − Pink
- V Fuchsia
- ▲ Purple

CARNATION

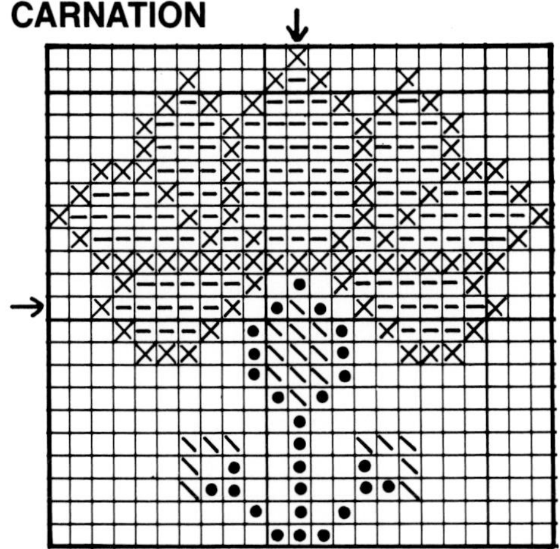

BASKET OF FRUIT

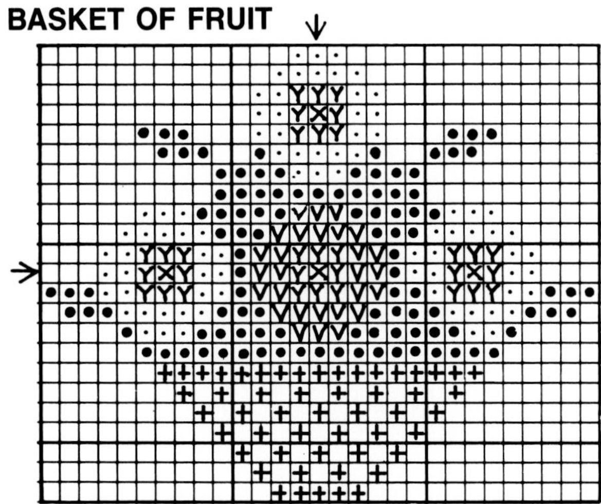

BLUEBIRDS

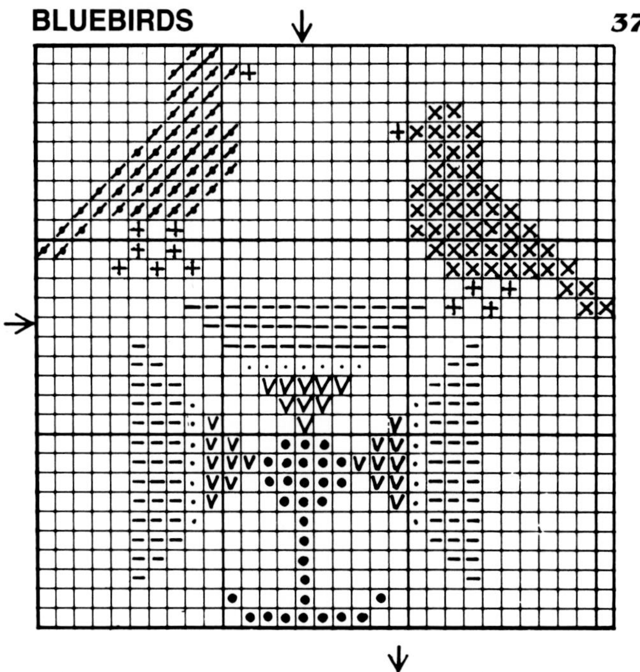

HEARTS AND FLOWERS

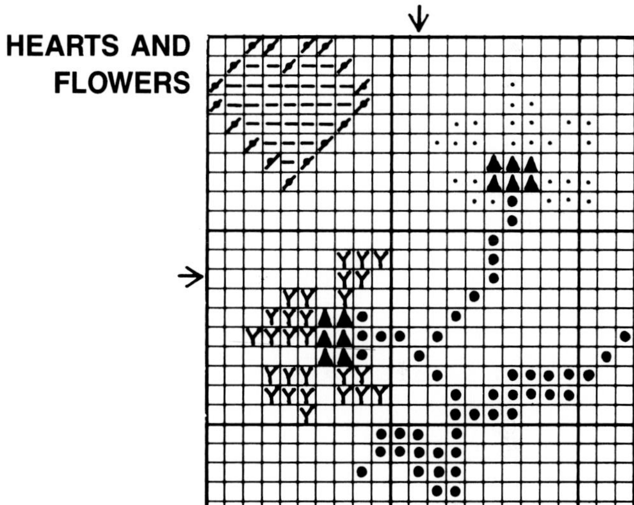

HEART AND STRAWBERRY

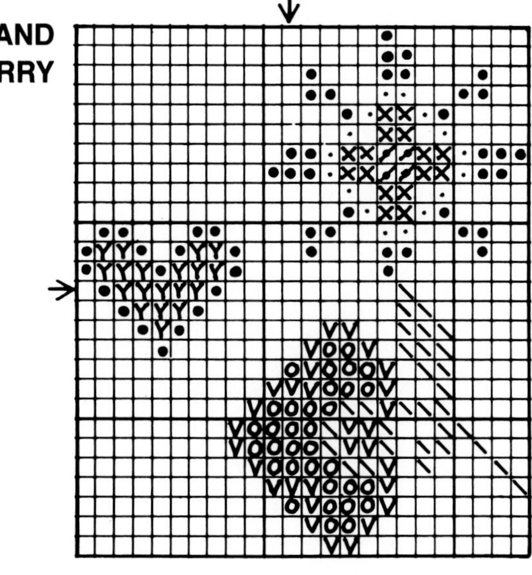

apples apples apples apples apples apples apples apples
ABCDEFGHIJKLMNOPQRSTU
VWXYZ AND 123456789
Apples and Trees & Blossoms and Bees
I love apples I love apples I love apples
Cobblers and Cakes and Strudels and Pies
Yummies for the Tummy, A Feast for the Eyes
designed and wrought by
merrily beams june 1974
apples apples apples apples apples apples apples

Fresh from the field...

Nature's bounty abounds, offering year-round goodness in cross-stitch.

- "Apples and Trees" Sampler
- "Welcome to My Kitchen" Sampler
- Flowering Strawberry
- "Whole Bunches" from the Earth
- Harvesting Apples and Pumpkins

opposite page: "Apples and Trees" Sampler

"Apples and Trees" Sampler

"Apples and Trees" Sampler achieves extra detail with two sizes of cross-stitches worked on even-weave fabric.

Sampler

SIZE:

Design area, approximately 8⅞″ × 12⅜″.

EQUIPMENT:

Tape measure. Scissors. Pencil. Embroidery hoop (optional). Tapestry needle. **For blocking and mounting:** Soft wooden board. Brown wrapping paper. Turkish towel. T-square. Ruler. Thumbtacks. Sewing and darning needles.

MATERIALS:

Off-white 23 or 24-count even-weave linen, piece 14″ × 18″. Six-strand embroidery floss: one 7-yard skein each light green, champagne, medium brown, black, rose, light blue; two each of brick red and dark green. Heavy mounting cardboard. Sewing thread to match linen. Frame.

DIRECTIONS:

Read Cross-Stitch How-To's, page 177. Each square on chart represents one thread of fabric. Larger crosses are worked over two threads, smaller crosses over one thread. Use three strands of floss in needle for large crosses; use two strands of floss for small crosses. Place linen on a smooth, hard surface so that long edges are at sides. Measure 2⅞″ down from top edge and 2½″ in from left edge; mark intersection of fabric threads with a pin, for first stitch. To prevent raveling, tape edges with masking tape.

Thread tapestry needle with 18″ to 20″ length of floss, using number of strands indicated above. Follow chart and color key to cross-stitch sampler, beginning at pin on fabric with top of leaf in upper left corner of chart.

To personalize sampler, use letters from the sampler and the additional lower case letters from the chart.

Block and mount finished sampler following directions in Embroidery Basics, page 175. Frame as desired.

"APPLES AND TREES" SAMPLER

S Brick Red	Champagne
Dark Green	Light Green
Black	Rose
Light Blue	Medium Brown

apples apples apples apples apples apples apples apples
Apples and Trees
Blossoms and Bees

I love apples I love apples I love apples
Cobblers and Cakes and Strudels and Pies
Yummies for the Tummy, A Feast for the Eyes
designed and wrought by
merrily beams june 1974
apples apples apples apples apples apples apples apples
abcdefghijklmnopqrstuvwxyz

"Welcome to My Kitchen" Sampler

Beets and carrots frame a homey motto—mount it in a bulletin board for a practical kitchen accessory.

"Welcome to My Kitchen"

SIZE:
Design area, 7½" × 6".

EQUIPMENT:
Ruler. Scissors. Tapestry needle.

MATERIALS:
White 18-count Aida fabric, piece 12" × 14". Susan Bates Anchor® embroidery floss, one skein white #1 and each color listed in color key, except two skeins fudge #380. Wheatland Crafts® Memo Board; for mail-order information, see Buyers' Guide, page 174).

DIRECTIONS:
Read Cross-Stitch How-To's, page 177. Prepare Aida cloth for embroidery. Place piece with long edges at top and bottom. Measure 3⅜" in and 3" down from upper right corner and mark fabric square for placement of first stitch. Work design in cross-stitch, following chart and color key, and using two strands of floss in tapestry needle; use two strands white floss in cup areas without symbols. Make each stitch over one square of fabric. Using backstitch, outline vegetables with two strands fudge floss; outline cup with two strands dark gray; for embroidery stitch detail, see page 178. When all embroidery is completed, press piece gently, face down, on padded surface. Mount needlework in memo board following manufacturer's instructions.

KITCHEN SAMPLER MEMO BOARD

- ⊡ Light Salmon #11
- ▲ Dark Salmon #13
- ⊟ Light Emerald #265
- ⊙ Medium Emerald #267
- ■ Dark Emerald #269
- Ⓤ Light Apricot #323
- ☑ Dark Apricot #326
- ☒ Fudge #380
- ⧄ Light Gray #398
- ⊞ Medium Gray #399
- ● Dark Gray #400

Flowering Strawberry Pillow

Plump strawberries adorn a small (8¾″ square) pillow; drawn thread techniques frame each delicious bunch.

Strawberry Pillow

SIZE:

Approximately 8¾″ square.

EQUIPMENT:

Ruler. Straight pins. Regular and embroidery scissors. Sewing needle. Tapestry needle. Small bodkin. Iron. Sewing machine.

MATERIALS:

White 22-count hardanger fabric, white broadcloth, and desired backing fabric (we used green and white checked gingham): one 10″ square each. DMC six-strand embroidery floss, one skein each: white, yellow #744, pink #3326, red #349, medium green #702, and dark green #699. DMC pearl cotton, medium green #702: one skein size 5, one ball size 8 (size 8 optional). White satin ribbon ⅛″ wide, 1 yard. Pregathered white lace ¾″ wide, 1⅛ yards. White thread. Fiberfill.

DIRECTIONS:

Working notes: Hardanger fabric is made up of 22 double threads-to-the-inch. Throughout these directions, illustrations, and charts on page 180, this double thread is referred to and shown as one thread. For additional stitch details, see page 178.

Drawing threads: Overcast edges of 10″-square hardanger piece (pillow front) to prevent raveling. Fold piece in half crosswise and lengthwise to locate center; mark with pin. Place piece wrong side up. Locate the center-most six threads running in one direction; slip a pin under these threads near center, and pull up; carefully snip them with embroidery scissors. Draw out threads on either side of center, working slowly as you approach fabric edges. Stop when drawn section measures 4″ from center point on either side. Trim thread ends to 1″ long; fold over onto fabric and tack down; do not stitch through to right side. Returning to center, draw out six threads in opposite direction, in same manner. There will be an open square in center of piece.

(continued)

Hemstitching: See details. Turn hardanger piece to right side. Separate strands of medium green floss and thread tapestry needle with two strands. Working from left to right along one drawn section, bring needle to right side, two threads below open area. Pass needle from right to left under first two exposed vertical threads (**Figure 1**). Pull floss snug, bundling fabric threads together; insert needle back into fabric two threads below drawn section and to the right of stitch just made (**Figure 2**). Continue in same manner to center square, then reverse piece and hemstitch opposite edge of same section, working from center out to edge. Repeat on remaining three sections.

Inserting Ribbon: See details. Cut two pieces of ribbon, each 10″ long. Turn hardanger piece to wrong side. At left end of horizontal hemstitched section, bring ¼″ end of ribbon up through fabric and wrap around the first group of hemstitched threads; slip-stitch end to ribbon, enclosing threads. Turn work to right side; thread free end of ribbon into bodkin. Working from right to left, pass bodkin over the next two groups of threads (a and b) and insert the point from left to right under a and over b (**Figure 1**). Twist a over b by inserting bodkin under b from right to left (**Figure 2**); pull ribbon through until taut. Repeat interlacing across work, skipping over center square and being careful to keep ribbon flat; fold ribbon end to wrong side and secure as for first end. Repeat along vertical section.

Cross-Stitch Embroidery: See chart. Read Cross-Stitch How-To's, page 177. Begin embroidery in lower left quarter of pillow front by counting nine threads down and eleven threads to the left of hemstitching; mark thread with pin for first stitch. Follow chart and color key to work motif, using one strand floss in needle and making each stitch over one thread of fabric. Begin at pin with stitch marked by arrow on chart.

When lower left quarter is completed, work lower right to correspond, counting nine threads down and eleven threads to the right for first stitch; work design in reverse.

For remaining quarters, reverse pillow front and repeat embroidery, following directions for first half.

(continued)

HEMSTITCHING

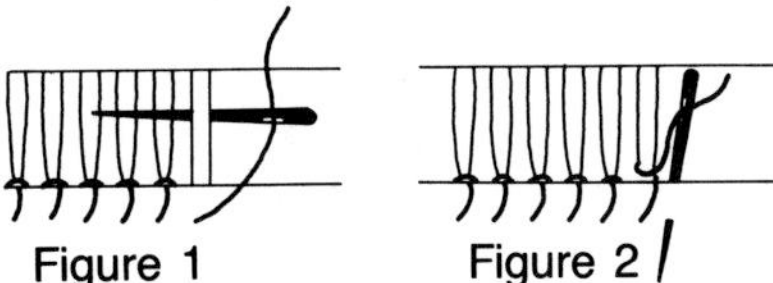
Figure 1 Figure 2

INSERTING RIBBON

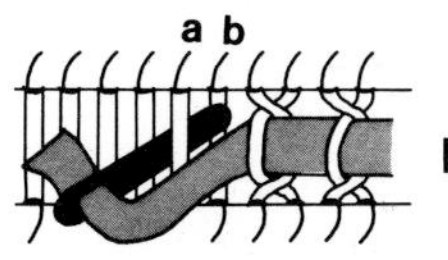

Figure 1

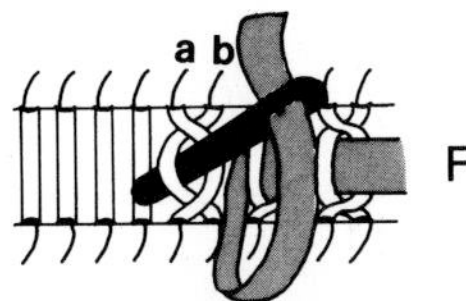

Figure 2

STRAWBERRY PILLOW

- ☒ Dark Green #699
- ⊟ Medium Green #702
- ● Red #349
- ▯ Pink #3326
- ⁚ Yellow #744
- ⧄ White

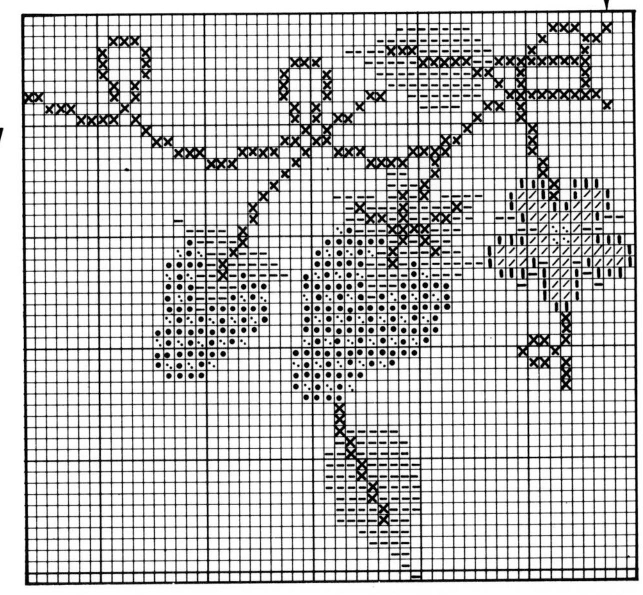

Hardanger Embroidery: Read hardanger directions and study details on page 180. Begin work in lower left quarter of pillow front by measuring 1¾″ down and 3⅛″ to the left of hemstitching; mark thread with a pin for first stitch of first Kloster block. Work Kloster blocks. After working blocks, use embroidery scissors to cut fabric threads indicated by black lines on chart A. Then pull out threads between blocks, leaving open squares and groups of horizontal and vertical threads; see chart B. When completed, work Woven Bars and Dove's Eyes as described on page 180.

Finishing: Press completed work well. Place white broadcloth, right side up, on a flat surface. Place embroidered pillow front, right side up, on broadcloth, matching edges; baste together ½″ from edges. Pin lace to edges of pillow front, placing right sides together and the gathering line of lace at basting; stitch together with ½″ seam. Pin pillow back to front, right sides together; stitch with ⅝″ seam, leaving an opening for turning. Turn to right side. Tie remaining ribbon into a bow and tack to pillow center. Stuff pillow with fiberfill; slip-stitch opening closed.

CHART A

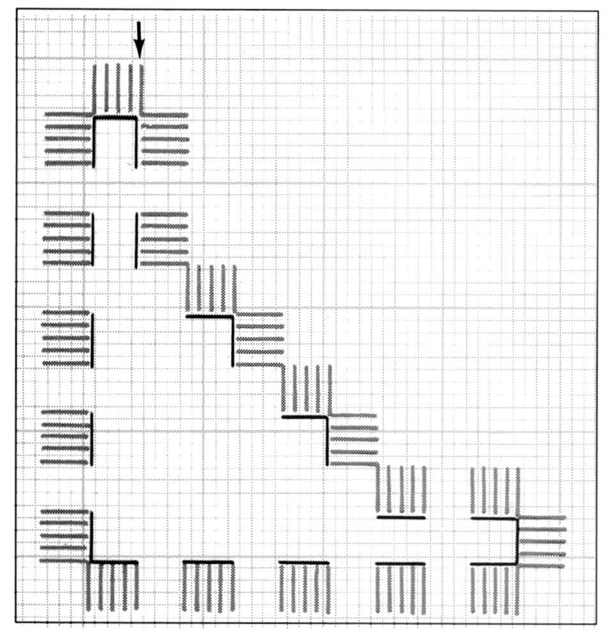

CHART B

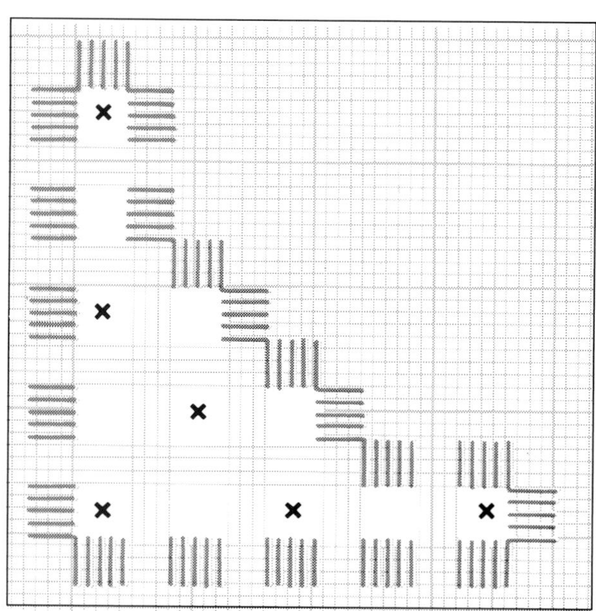

"Whole Bunches" from the Earth

Whole bunches—of fruits, veggies, even balloons—decorate an assortment of easy gifts. Stitch a pillow, sachet, bookmark, jar cover, or picture in less time than you might think.

Whole Bunches Pillow

SIZE:
9″ square, plus ruffle.

EQUIPMENT:
Masking tape. Sewing and tapestry needles. Embroidery hoop. Scissors. Sewing machine. Steam iron. Basting thread.

MATERIALS:
Ecru 14-count Aida fabric, piece 10″ square. DMC six-strand embroidery floss, one skein of each color listed in color key, plus one skein each of light coral #353, gold #782, and pale jade #772. Fabric for pillow back, 10″ square. Purchased stenciled edging 2½″ wide, two yards. Ecru sewing thread. Fiberfill.

DIRECTIONS:
Read Cross-Stitch How-To's, page 177. Tape Aida edges to prevent raveling. Fold fabric into quarter to find center lines and mark these lines with basting. Follow chart and color key to work design: Symbols on chart represent cross-stitches, lines indicate half cross-stitch and backstitch. Work each stitch over one square of fabric threads. Beginning at center, work cross-stitches first, using three strands of floss in needle. Work remaining stitches as follows:

Grapes: Using two strands of floss in needle, backstitch (see stitch details, page 178) left and middle stems with brown, right stem with gold.

Balloons: Using two strands of floss, backstitch strings with gold.

Asparagus: Using three strands of floss, work top of left and right spears with medium green half cross-stitches, top of middle spear with light green half cross-stitches; using two strands, backstitch ribbon with light coral.

Carrots: Using three strands of floss, work half cross-stitches: use pale jade for the uppermost four stitches and one strand of medium green together with two strands of light green in needle for left carrot top; work middle carrot top with medium green; work uppermost six stitches of right carrot top with light and medium green as for left top, then complete carrot top with light green. *Note:* Refer to color photograph if unsure of colors.

Bananas: Using two strands of floss in needle, backstitch lines with gold.

When embroidery is completed, remove basting and tape, and press

(continued)

I LOVE YOU
WHOLE
BUNCHES

piece gently on wrong side. To finish pillow, join ends of edging with right sides facing, forming a ring. Gather ring along unfinished edge to 38″. With right sides facing, pin edging to pillow front, matching raw edges; baste layers together ½″ from edges. Pin pillow back to pillow front with right sides facing, enclosing ruffle. Sew together with a ¼″ seam, leaving an opening along bottom for turning. Turn piece right side out, remove basting, stuff firmly, then slip-stitch opening closed.

WHOLE BUNCHES PILLOW

- Brown #839
- Forest Green #3345
- Medium Green #905
- Red #666
- Dark Green #987
- Violet #915
- Plum #326
- Jade #3348
- Light Green #907
- Medium Pink #605
- Turquoise #959
- Dark Pink #602
- Orange #970
- Light Yellow #3078
- Medium Yellow #676

Sachets

SIZE:

Each, 4″ square, plus ruffle.

EQUIPMENT:

See Whole Bunches Pillow.

MATERIALS:

For each: Ecru 14-count Aida fabric, piece 6″ square. Fabric for back, 5″ square. White pregathered eyelet edging ¾″ wide, ½ yard. DMC six-strand embroidery floss, small amount; see Whole Bunches Pillow color key and chart. Ecru sewing thread. Satin ribbon 1/16″ wide, ⅝ yard. Purchased potpourri.

DIRECTIONS:

Read Cross-Stitch How-To's, page 177. Tape fabric, mark centers, and work embroidery as for Whole Bunches Pillow, following the same chart; center (first) stitch of each motif is indicated by arrow on chart. When embroidery is completed, remove basting and tape, then press embroidered piece on wrong side.

With ribbon threaded in tapestry needle, work running stitches over two, then under two fabric threads between the 19th and 20th fabric threads from each edge all around motif; begin and end at center top, then tie ribbon ends in a bow. Complete sachet as for Whole Bunches Pillow, attaching eyelet as for gathered stenciled edging. Stuff sachet with potpourri before slip-stitching the opening closed.

I LOVE YOU
WHOLE
BUNCHES

Jam Jar Covers

SIZE:
Each, 7½" square.

EQUIPMENT:
Masking tape. Scissors. Straight pins. Zigzag sewing machine. Sewing needle. Tapestry needle. Embroidery hoop (optional). Steam iron.

MATERIALS:
For four different covers: Yellow 29-count even-weave fabric, ½ yard. Coats & Clark Royal Mouliné six-strand embroidery floss, one skein of each color listed in color key. Matching and contrasting sewing thread. Brown satin ribbon ⅛" wide, 2 yards.

DIRECTIONS:
Read Cross-Stitch How-To's, page 177. Cut four 7½"-square pieces of fabric. Tape fabric edges to prevent raveling. Fold each fabric square into quarters; mark horizontal and vertical center lines with pins. Using contrasting thread, baste along vertical and horizontal center lines. These lines correspond to arrows on charts. Using three strands of floss and working each stitch over a "square" of three fabric threads, work designs following charts and color key, beginning in center. Press embroidery on wrong side. Remove tape and zigzag-stitch around each piece ½" from edge. Using a straight pin, pull out threads as far as stitching to create fringe. Cut ribbon into four equal lengths and use to tie covers around jars.

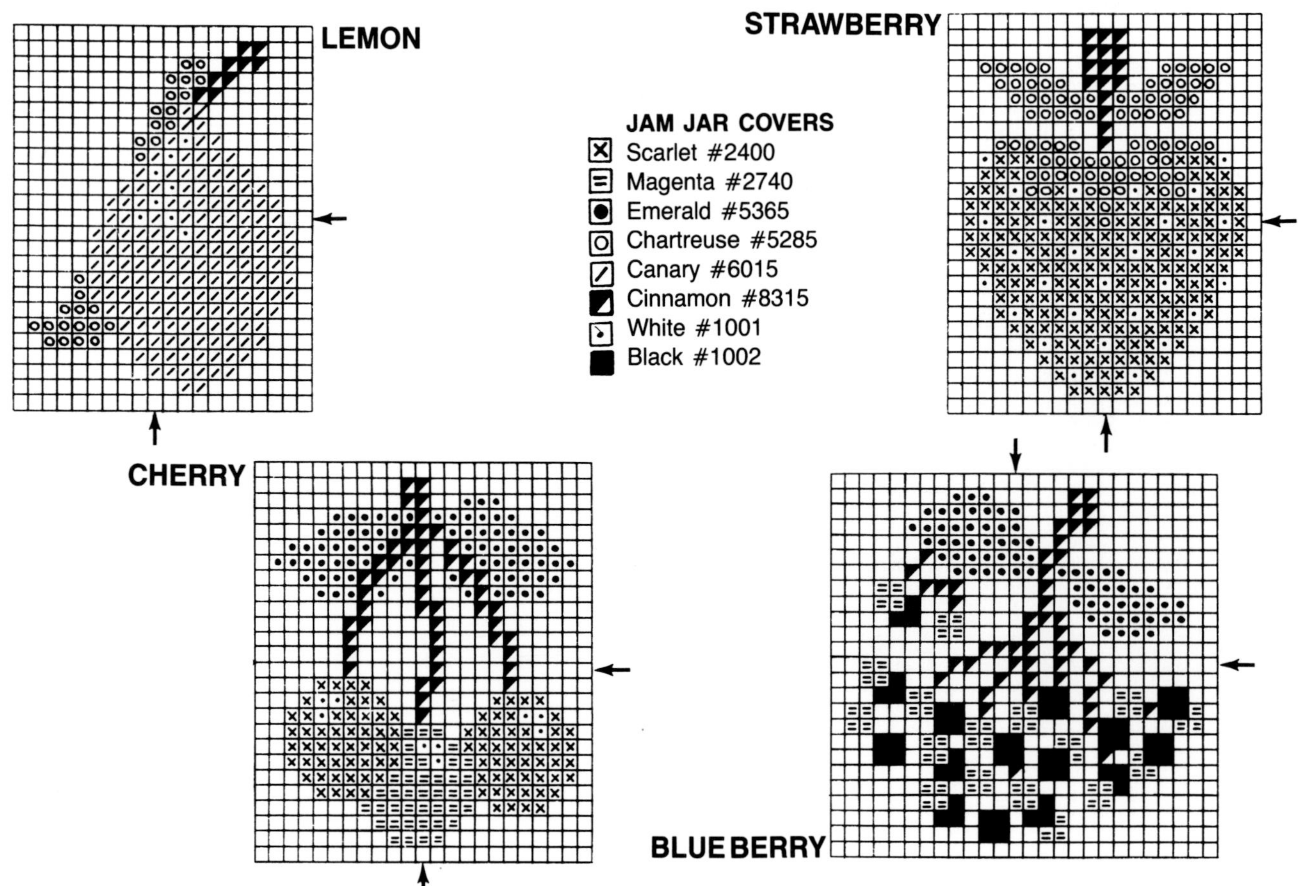

Wild Roses Picture

SIZE:
Design area, 5″ × 6″.

EQUIPMENT:
Masking tape. Ruler. Straight pin. Tapestry needle. Embroidery scissors. Small embroidery hoop. Steam iron.

MATERIALS:
Off-white 22-count hardanger fabric, piece 9″ × 10″. DMC six-strand embroidery floss, one skein of each color listed in color key.

DIRECTIONS:
Read Cross-Stitch How-To's, page 177. Tape edges of fabric to prevent raveling. Place fabric with longer edges at sides. Measure 2⅞″ in from left edge and 2″ down from top; mark intersecting fabric threads with a pin, for first stitch. Separating floss and using four strands in needle, work design in cross-stitch, following chart and color key; begin at pin, with stitch indicated by arrow on chart. Each symbol on chart represents one cross-stitch, worked over a square of two horizontal and two vertical fabric threads.

When embroidery is completed, remove tape and steam-press piece on wrong side over a padded surface. Frame as desired.

WILD ROSE PICTURE

- ⊠ Medium Green #906
- ☒ Light Green#3348
- ◢ Dark Brown #315
- ⧗ Dark Antique Rose #221
- ⁘ Medium Antique Rose #356
- ▯ Yellow #973
- ⊡ Dark Rose #3328
- ▨ Medium Rose #353
- ○ Cream #948
- ⊻ Pink #335

Morning Glory and Pansy Initial Bookmarks

SIZE:

Each, approximately 14″ long.

EQUIPMENT:

Masking tape. Ruler. Tapestry needle. Straight pin. Scissors. Mat knife. Small embroidery hoop. Pencil.

MATERIALS:

For each: White 22-count hardanger fabric, 8″ × 10″ piece. DMC six-strand embroidery floss, small amounts of colors listed in color key. Green grosgrain ribbon ⅜″ wide, 11″. Stiff cardboard. White craft glue.

DIRECTIONS:

For each: Read Cross-Stitch How-To's, page 177. Tape fabric edges to prevent raveling. With pencil, mark two 3½″ squares and two 2″ squares on fabric, making sure that fabric threads run horizontally and vertically. Measuring in both directions on one of each size square, find center thread; mark this thread with pin.

Work desired flower in cross-stitch in the large square, following chart and color key. Separating floss and using two strands in tapestry needle, work each cross-stitch over a square of two horizontal and two vertical fabric threads; begin at center of motif, indicated on chart by arrows. Work initial on smaller marked square in same way; to find center of your initial, mark rectangle around chart to "box" design, then count squares along horizontal and vertical edges.

When embroidery is finished, mark a rectangle around each motif, leaving a ½″ margin beyond outermost stitches. Cut out piece along new lines. Cut and trim unworked squares to correspond. With pin, carefully ravel edges of each piece to create fringe about 3⁄16″ wide. Using mat knife and ruler, cut one piece of cardboard 3⁄16″ smaller all around than each fringed pair.

To create bookmark, glue a cardboard piece to back of each embroidered piece. Glue one end of ribbon to each cardboard, with ribbon extending below floral embroidery and above initial; be careful not to twist ribbon. Glue remaining fabric pieces to other side of cardboard, matching edges and covering ribbon ends.

MORNING GLORY

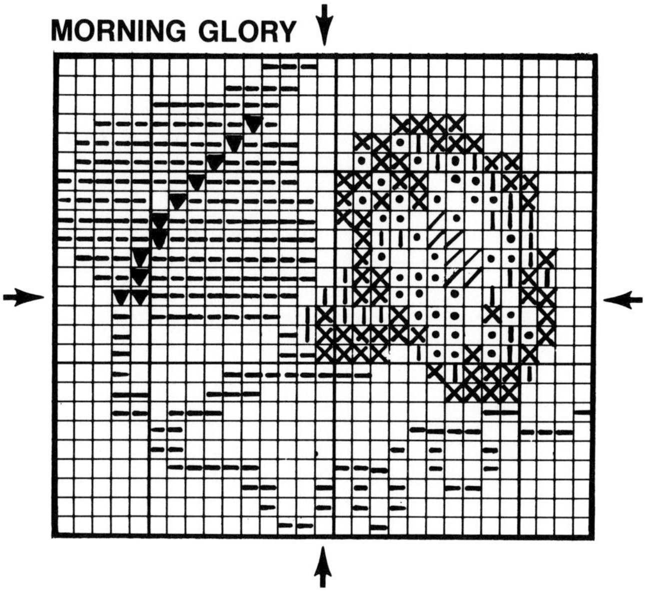

MORNING GLORY

- Turquoise #995
- Medium Blue #916
- Light Blue #828
- Medium Green #905
- Light Green #907
- Yellow #742

PANSY

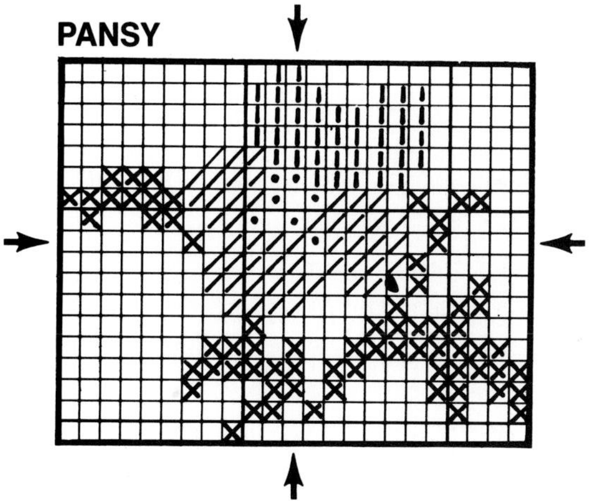

PANSY

- Black #310
- Violet #550
- Medium Green #905
- Light Orange #741

INITIAL CHART

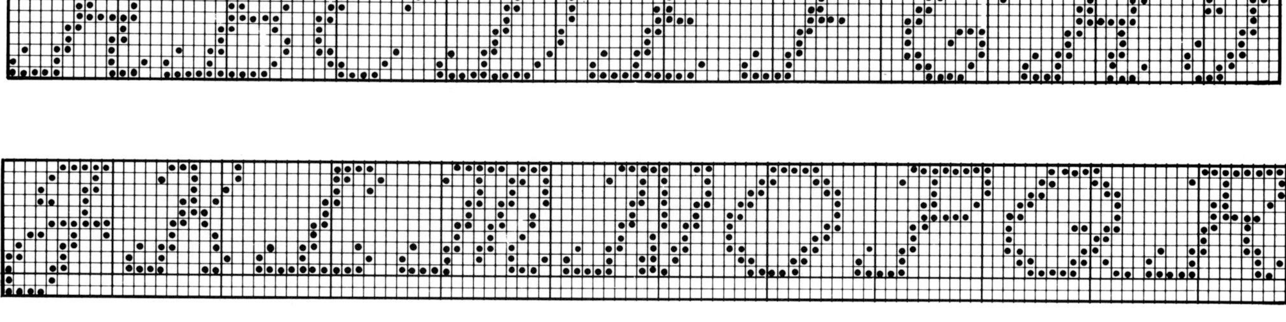

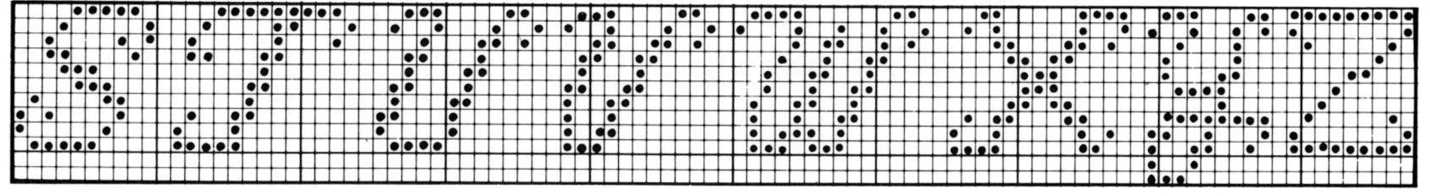

Harvesting Apples and Pumpkins

Harvesttime provides the inspiration for a sweet set of pictures. The apples and pumpkins look almost good enough to eat!

Harvest Scenes

SIZE:
Each design area, approximately 6¾" square.

EQUIPMENT:
Embroidery and regular scissors. Tapestry and sewing needles. Dark-colored sewing thread. Embroidery hoop. Steam iron.

MATERIALS:
For each: Charles Craft 14-count "Fiddler's Cloth," piece 11" square; for mail order information, see Buyers' Guide, page 174. Susan Bates Anchor® six-strand embroidery floss, one skein each color listed in color key. Pearl cotton size 5, one ball white.

(continued)

DIRECTIONS:

For each: (If making both designs, make sure that "straight" or grain of fabric runs in the same direction for each.) Read Cross-Stitch How-To's, page 177, before beginning. Prepare fabric as directed. To determine center of fabric, baste a line from center of one side to center of opposite side; baste a second line from center of third side to center of fourth side; basting lines will cross at center.

Place fabric in hoop. Beginning at center stitch marked by arrows on chart, work design following chart and color key. Each symbol on chart rep-

HARVESTING APPLES AND PUMPKINS

- Peach #06
- Rust #326
- Blue #779
- Brass #874
- Terra-Cotta #341
- *Brown #355
- *Red #47
- **Orange #316
- Gold #307
- Burgundy #20
- Grass Green #246
- Lime Green #254
- White #1
- Black #403

*For apple design only.
**For pumpkin design only.

resents one cross-stitch (apron and kerchief are worked with one strand white pearl cotton and half cross-stitch); different symbols represent different colors. Solid lines indicate backstitches. See stitch details, page 178. Using two strands floss in needle throughout, work each cross-stitch over one horizontal and one vertical thread or "square" of fabric. Work backstitches last, using two strands rust for inner pumpkin lines and two strands black for all else.

After all embroidery is completed, remove fabric from hoop and steam-press gently on wrong side. Mount and frame as desired.

Country friends...

No country setting would be complete without an occasional visitor.

- Napping Kittens
- Bashful Hare
- Spring's Cottontail
- Summer's Songbird
- Fall's Squirrel
- Winter's Sparrow
- Swan and Lily Pad
- Chickadee on an Oak Branch
- Woodland Animals

opposite page: Napping Kittens

Napping Kittens

Napping kittens, framed in eyelet ruffles, snuggle on these dainty pillows.

Napping Kittens

SIZE:
Each pillow, approximately 10½″ square, plus trim.

EQUIPMENT:
Ruler. Straight pin. Scissors. Tapestry needle. Embroidery hoop (optional).

MATERIALS:
For each pillow: Pale green or blue 11-count Aida fabric, 12″ square. Desired backing fabric (we used blue poplin), 12″ square. White pregathered eyelet trim 2½″ wide, 1¼ yards. Matching sewing thread. DMC six-strand embroidery floss, one skein each color listed in color key, unless otherwise noted in parentheses. Pillow form, 10″ square.

DIRECTIONS:
Read Cross-Stitch How-To's, page 177. Prepare Aida for embroidery. To begin, measure 3″ up and 3″ in from lower right corner of fabric; mark point with pin. Move pin two fabric "squares" to the left for "Cat on Fence", five squares to the left for "Cat on Steps". Begin stitching at pin, starting at left edge of dark rust brick just inside border design. Each symbol on chart represents one cross-stitch; different symbols represent different colors. Work small symbols over one square of Aida; work large outlined symbols over four squares for full stitch, two squares for half stitch.

Medium-weight solid lines separate color areas; work symboled colors first, then fill in blank areas within outlines as directed below. Ignore heavy solid lines until all cross-stitching is completed; these lines indicate additional embroidery. For embroidery stitch details, see page 178.

Cat on Steps

Fill in blank flower areas with cross-stitch, using medium blue-violet for upper left flower pot and light rose for upper right pot; along left edge, use powder blue in foliage below climbing roses, pale yellow in lower left corner; working to right, fill in next area with periwinkle, then the next with avocado. When all cross-stitching is completed, work additional embroidery with three strands floss: Work medium blue-green "shadow" lines in backstitch as charted along steps and pillar. Work avocado stem at top of climbing roses and black cat's eyes in straight stitch. Satin-stitch cat's tongue with light rose as shown.

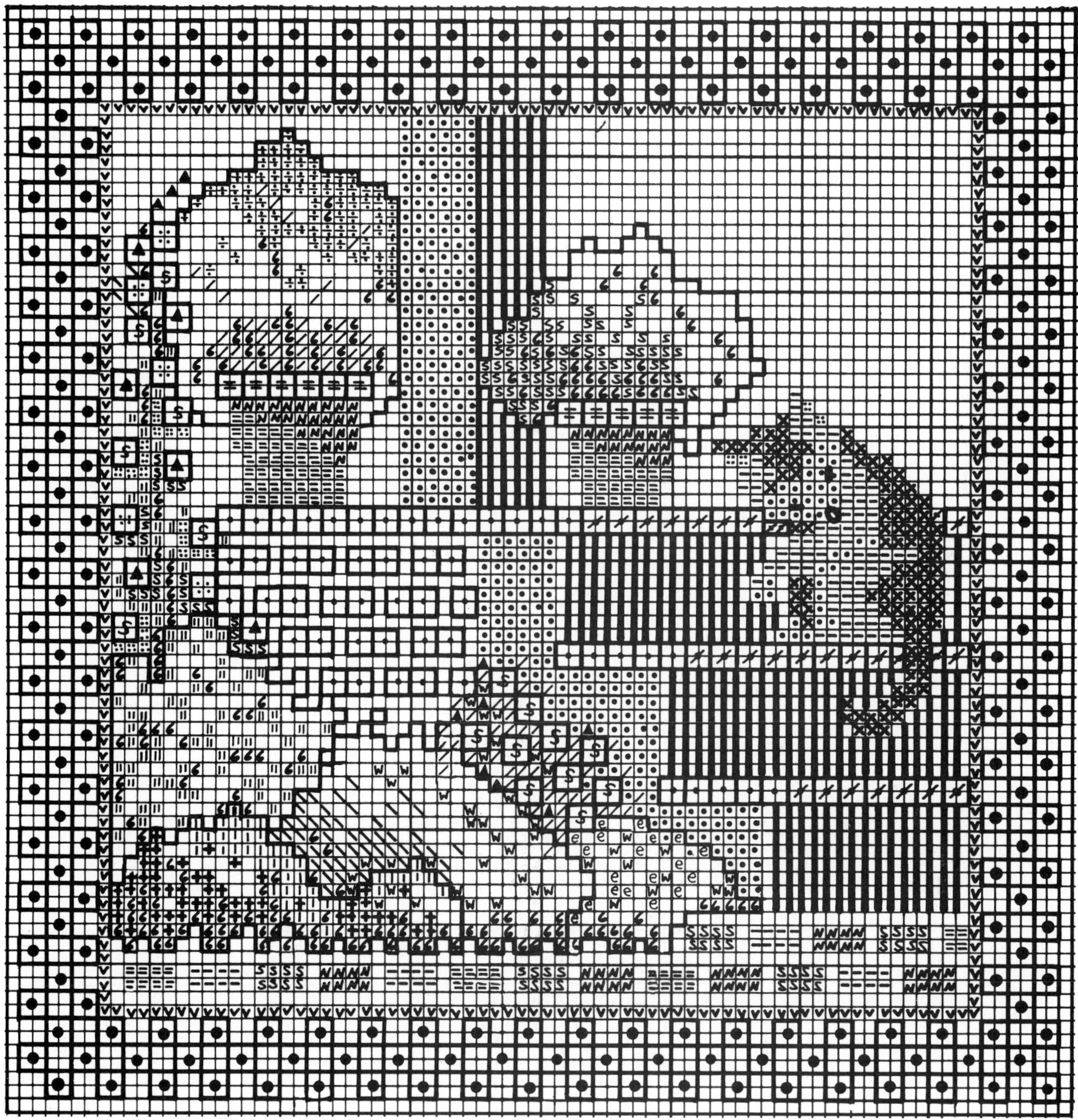

CAT ON STEPS

- White (2)
- Light Rust #922
- Dark Rust #918
- Mint Green #369
- Avocado #470
- Emerald Green #561
- Bottle Green #501
- Light Rose #963
- Medium Rose #962
- Dark Rose #961
- Periwinkle #341
- Medium Blue-Violet #793
- Powder Blue #827
- Light Blue-Green #928
- Medium Blue-Green #927 (2)
- Dark Blue-Green #926 (2)
- Pale Yellow #746
- Light Yellow #745
- Medium Yellow #743
- Nutmeg #436
- Black #310

Cat on Fence

Shown on page 62

Fill in blank areas with cross-stitch, using white for fence and cat; for flower areas, working left to right, fill in upper tier with sky blue, medium blue-violet, and mint green; fill in lower tier with medium blue-violet, light rose, and avocado. When all cross-stitching is completed, work additional embroidery: Using three strands medium blue-green, make straight-stitch "shadows" on lattice border. Using two strands medium yellow, make French knot center for each large powder blue flower. Work black cat's eyes in straight stitch; work a light rose cat's nose with French knot or satin stitch as desired.

Finishing: Steam-press completed embroidery, right side up, on a very well-padded surface. Assemble pillow following directions in Sewing Hints, page 181; include eyelet trim in ¾″ seam.

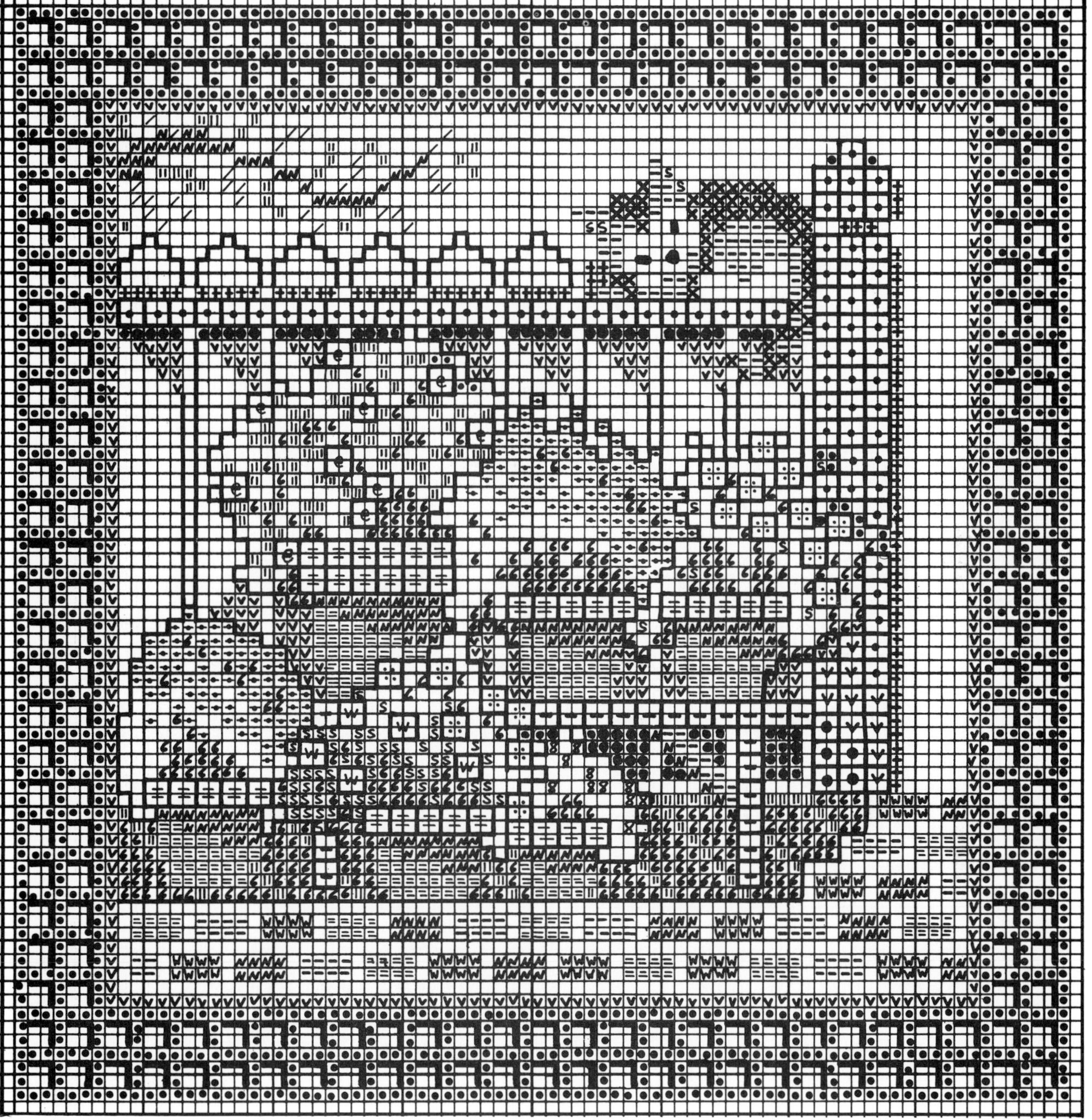

CAT ON FENCE

- White (4)
- Light Rust #922
- Dark Rust #918
- Mint Green #369
- Avocado #470
- Bottle Green #501
- Light Rose #963
- Medium Rose #962
- Salmon #760
- Periwinkle #341
  Medium Blue-Violet #793
- Powder Blue #827
  Sky Blue #813
- Light Blue-Green #928
- Medium Blue-Green #927
- Dark Blue-Green #926
- Medium Yellow #743
- Nutmeg #436
- Black #310

Bashful Hare Lap Robe

Surrounded by autumn leaves, a bashful hare peers out at the world. Lap robe is made from special polyacrylic fabric for easy care.

Lap Robe

SIZE:

35″ × 43″, plus self-fringe.

EQUIPMENT:

Ruler. Scissors. Straight pin. Embroidery hoop. Sewing machine. Steam iron. Tapestry needle. Basting thread. Air-soluble or water-erasable marking pen.

MATERIALS:

Zweigart® "Gloria" 100% polyacrylic fabric (article #7517), 55″ wide, one 54″-long panel, cream; to order from Hansi's Haus, see Buyers' Guide, page 174. Matching sewing thread. Susan Bates Anchor® six-strand embroidery floss, number of 8-meter skeins noted in parentheses after each color number listed in color key.

DIRECTIONS:

Read Cross-Stitch How-To's, page 177. Overcast raw edges of fabric to prevent raveling. Baste across large center panel in both directions with contrasting thread, to mark center point.

Place piece on work surface with longer edges of woven-in panels at sides. From marked center, measure 6¾″ up and 2½″ to the right; mark thread with pin for first stitch. For center panel, use six strands floss in tapestry needle, making each stitch over a "square" of two horizontal and two vertical fabric threads; leave eye areas unworked until remainder of motif is completed. When moving from one area of center design to another, be sure to count two threads for each blank square on chart. When center motif is completed, work eyes, following separate chart; use *two* strands of floss and work each stitch over *one* fabric thread. Use six strands of floss to work backstitching, indicated by solid lines on chart: outline rabbit with black, work remaining backstitching in coffee; for stitch detail, see page 178.

(continued)

CENTER MOTIF CHART

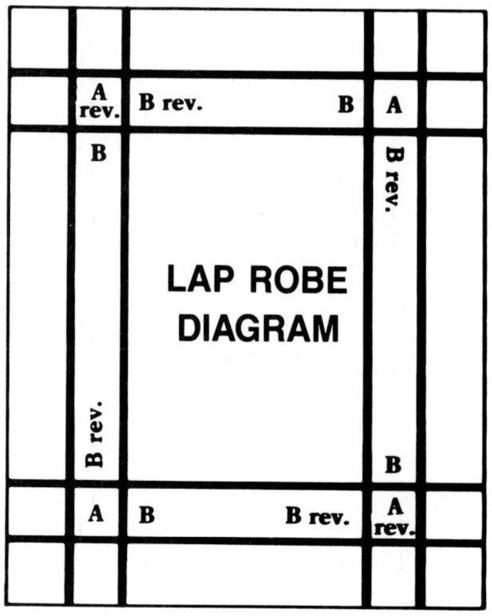

LAP ROBE DIAGRAM

A rev. | B rev. | B | A

B | B rev.

B rev. | B

A | B | B rev. | A rev.

EYE CHART

LAP ROBE CENTER MOTIF

- Light Salmon #9 (2)
- Medium Salmon #10 (2)
- Dark Apricot #326 (4)
- Terra Cotta #341 (3)
- Light Bark #347 (2)
- Dark Bark #349 (2)
- Linen #926 (2)
- Light Fawn #376 (3)
- Medium Fawn #379 (4)
- Dark Fawn #936 (2)
- Coffee #360 (5)
- Blue Mist #850 (4)
- Sea Blue #978 (2)
- Light Olive #280 (3)
- Dark Olive #924 (4)
- Light Topaz #306 (4)
- Dark Topaz #308 (3)
- Black #403 (1)

Referring to lap robe diagram and Charts A and B, embroider corners of woven-in border; squares on charts correspond to squares in the fabric border, for easier placement of first stitches: Start at lower left corner square, with Chart A; then work Chart B in border strip to the right for right "leg." To complete corner, work Chart B in reverse for left "leg." Invert lap robe and work upper right corner same as lower left. For remaining corners, work Chart A in reverse for corner, Chart B in reverse for left "leg," Chart B as is for right "leg."

Use two strands of floss for cross-stitches, working them over one fabric thread; use two strands of coffee for backstitching.

Hand-wash piece, if necessary; press on a well-padded surface. Using yardstick and air-soluble or water-erasable marking pen, draw lines 2½" and 5" beyond outermost band of woven border. Set sewing machine for fine stitch length; stitch around robe on inner line. Remove pen markings, if using water-soluble pen. Cut fabric along outer line. Ravel fabric threads to machine-stitching, forming self-fringe.

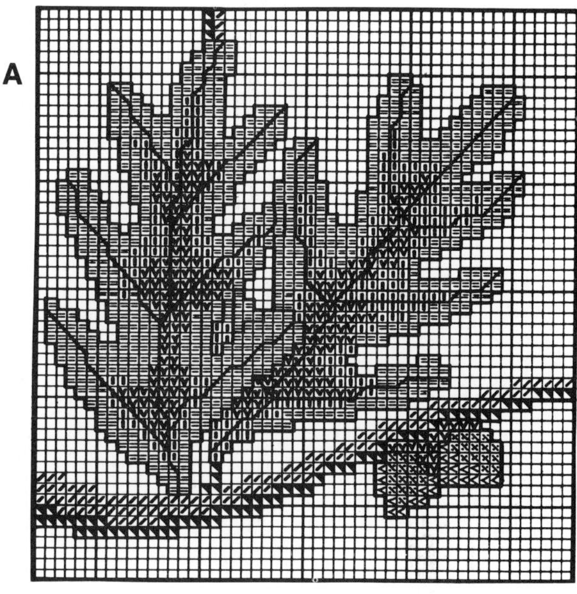

BORDER CHARTS

- Dark Apricot #326
- Terra Cotta #341
- Light Bark #347
- Dark Bark #349
- Coffee #360
- Blue Mist #850
- Light Topaz #306

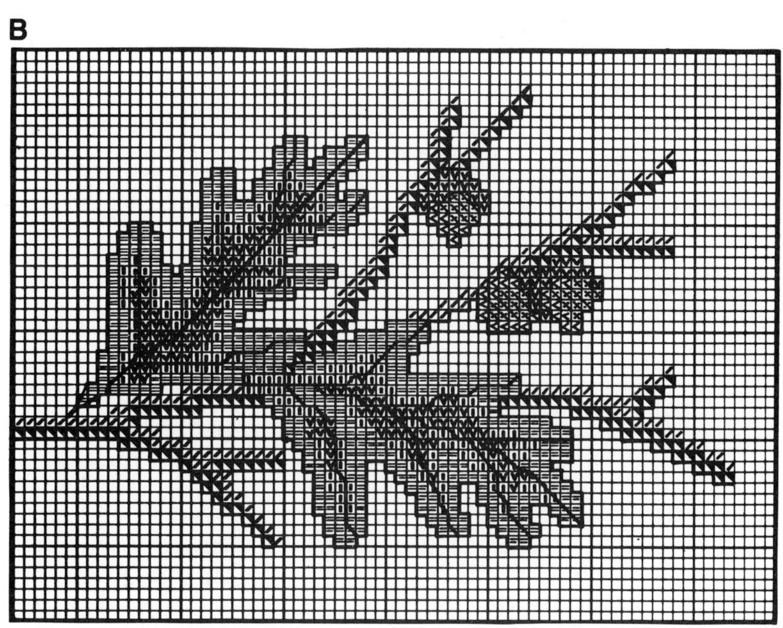

Spring's Cottontail
Summer's Songbird
Fall's Squirrel
Winter's Sparrow

Seasonal scenes are a pretty grouping for wall decor. Frame them in wooden hoops for a country touch.

Four Seasons Set

SIZE:
Each scene fits in 6"-diameter hoop.

EQUIPMENT:
Ruler. Scissors. Masking tape. Straight pins. Tapestry needle. Steam iron. Small paintbrush (optional).

MATERIALS:
For all: White 11-count Aida fabric, four 9"-square pieces. Susan Bates Anchor® embroidery floss: Two skeins light green #254; one skein each white #2, light blue #128, medium blue #131, yellow #302, medium green #256, dark green #246, medium red #47, dark red #5968, gray #398, light brown #308, medium brown #310, light beige #361, medium beige #362, pink #74, black #403. Four 6"-diameter wooden framing hoops. Stiff white cardboard, piece 12" square. Green dotted grosgrain ribbon 3/8" wide, one yard. Blue acrylic paint (optional). White craft glue.

DIRECTIONS:
Read Cross-Stitch How-To's, page 177. For each scene, find center of one (top) edge of 9" Aida piece; measure 2 5/8" down from center and mark fabric "square" with pin, for first stitch. Tape edges of piece to prevent raveling. Place piece in framing hoop. Separating floss and using three strands in tapestry needle, work scene in cross-stitch; to stitch, follow color chart on page 74. Each square on charts represents one square of fabric. Beginning at top stitch of top yellow flower, work a cross-stitch over one fabric square for each colored square of chart. As you stitch, disregard lines and dots on chart; however, when a line divides a square into two colors, work only a small half stitch from corner to center of square in each color, for a neat outline. When cross-stitching is complete, work backstitches between

(continued)

squares, following lines on chart; use one strand of floss to outline buildings, animals, and entire scene; use two or three strands for other details. Using three strands of floss, work French knots indicated by dots on chart; see stitch details, page 178.

When all embroidery is complete, remove piece from hoop; steam-press gently on a padded surface. For backing, trace around inner edge of hoop on cardboard. Cut out cardboard circle. If desired, paint hoop blue; let dry. Replace embroidered piece in hoop, centering scene. Place cardboard circle in hoop, covering back of embroidery, then fold excess fabric onto cardboard, trim, and tape in place. Cut 9″ length of grosgrain ribbon, tie into bow, and glue to brass hanger, below loop.

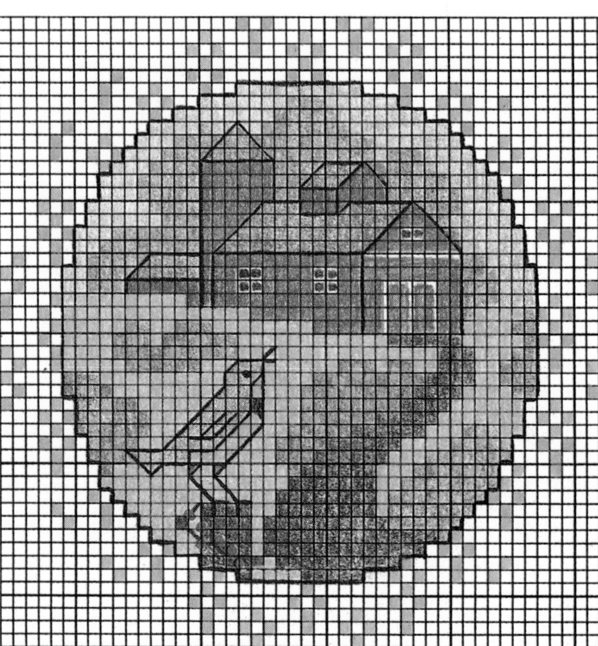

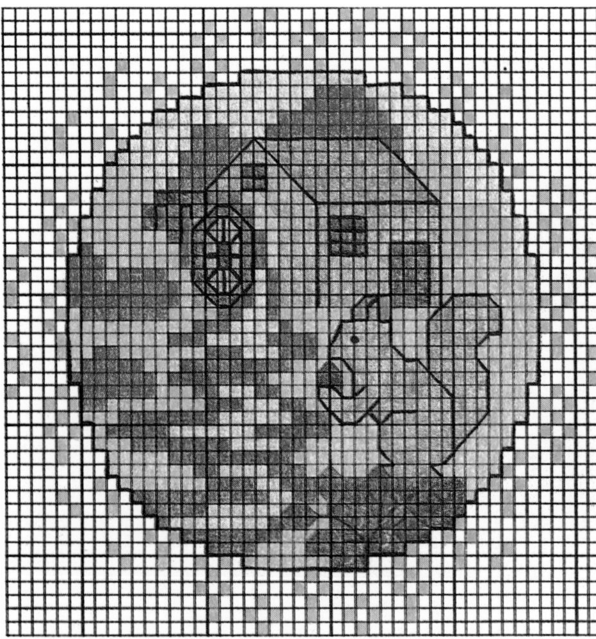

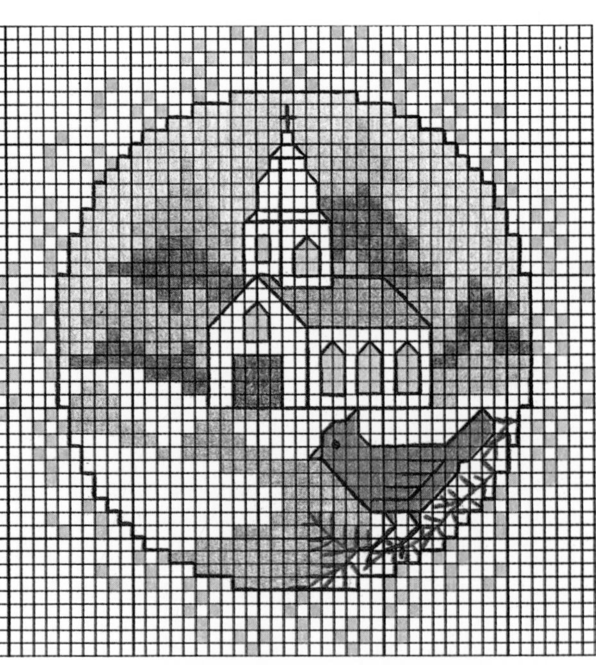

Swan and Lily Pad

A swan glides gracefully among water lilies. A simple hearts-and-flowers border completes the design for this charming pillow.

Swan Pillow

SIZE:

Approximately 12½″ square, plus ruffle.

EQUIPMENT:

Ruler. Masking tape. Straight pins. Scissors. Tapestry and sewing needles. Embroidery hoop. Steam iron. Sewing machine.

MATERIALS:

White 11-count Aida fabric, piece at least 17″ square. DMC six-strand embroidery floss, one skein each color listed in color key, except two skeins dark aqua #958. Cotton fabrics 45″ wide: light aqua, ½ yard; light pink, ⅜ yard. White flat lace trim ⅜″ wide, 3 yards. Fiberfill.

DIRECTIONS:

Read Cross-Stitch How-To's, page 177. Prepare Aida cloth for embroidery. Measure 3⅛″ in and down from upper left corner and mark for placement of first stitch. Work border and center design in cross-stitch, following chart and color key and using three strands floss in needle. When cross-stitching is complete, outline swan with backstitch, using two strands dark gray floss; see stitch detail, page 178. When all embroidery is complete, press piece gently face down on padded surface.

To assemble pillow, place embroidery face up on a flat surface. Measure and mark on Aida a 13½″ square (or 1⅜″ margin) around design; trim on marked lines. Cut 13½″ pillow back from aqua fabric. For ruffles, cut 6″-wide light aqua strip and 4½″-wide light pink strip, each three yards long; piece as necessary. Fold aqua ruffle in half lengthwise and press; stitch lace to right side of ruffle along folded edge. Assemble ruffles and construct pillow as directed in Sewing Hints, page 181 so that pink ruffle is in front of light aqua ruffle.

SWAN AND LILY PAD PILLOW

- ⊡ Light Aqua #964
- V Dark Aqua #958 (2)
- ⧄ Light Green #704
- ☒ Dark Green #701
- I Light Pink #605
- ● Dark Pink #961
- S Lavender #554
- ✚ Light Orange #740
- ⊟ Light Gray #318
- ▲ Dark Gray #413

Chickadee on an Oak Branch

Little chickadee sits on an oak branch, watching the autumn leaves turn bright colors. Pillow measures 14" square, plus the ruffle.

Chickadee Pillow

SIZE:
14" square, plus ruffle.

EQUIPMENT:
Tapestry needle. Scissors. Basting thread. Embroidery hoop (optional). Steam Iron.

MATERIALS:
Zweigart® 14-count Fine Aida fabric, one 15" square, color #740 Parchment. Susan Bates Anchor® six-strand embroidery floss, one skein each color listed in color key, unless otherwise noted in parentheses. Dark gray chintz 44" wide (or other desired fabric for back and ruffle), ⅝ yard. Matching sewing thread. Knife-edge pillow form 14" square.

DIRECTIONS:
Read Cross-Stitch How-To's, page 177; prepare Aida as directed. With contrasting thread, baste across cloth in both directions to mark center point.

From center point, count two squares to the left and one square down; begin work here with black stitch indicated by arrow on chart. Using two strands floss in tapestry needle, work design in cross-stitch, following chart and color key and working each stitch over one square of fabric. For oak leaves, work center section, then fill in outer section with the lighter value of leaf's center color, referring to color photograph if necessary; work medium tangerine around the terra cotta centers.

When cross-stitching is complete, work backstitch stems, leaf veins, and outlines as indicated by solid lines on chart, using two strands of floss: Use black for bird, medium loden green for ferns, and dark fudge for remaining work. Using two strands of blaze and light tangerine floss, work French knots for bittersweet berries, alternating colors randomly. For stitch details, see page 178.

Remove basting threads; press completed embroidery on a well-padded surface. From chintz, cut a 15" square (pillow back) and a 5½" × 120" strip (ruffle), piecing as necessary. Assemble pillow with ruffle as directed in Sewing Hints, page 181.

CHICKADEE ON AN OAK BRANCH

- ⊡ White #1
- ⊞ Light Burgundy #19
- Dark Burgundy #22
- Light Loden Green #260
- Medium Loden Green #261
- Light Topaz #305
- Medium Topaz #306
- Light Tangerine #314*
- Blaze #335*
- Medium Tangerine #925
- Terra Cotta #340
- Fawn #936 (2)
- Dark Fudge #381 (2)
- Gray #400
- Black #403

*French Knot Berries

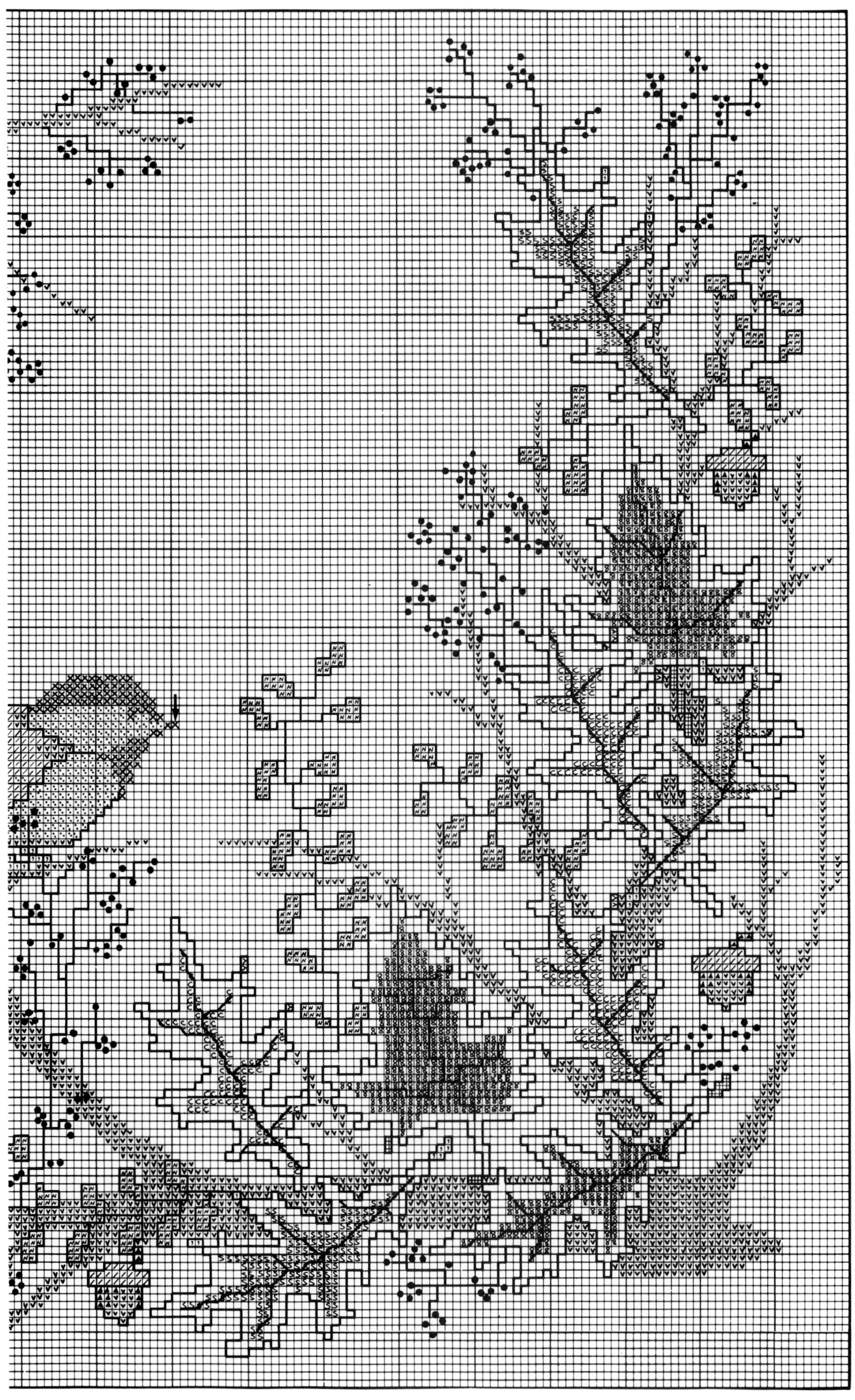

Woodland Animals

Whether you stitch just one or all four, petite woodland scenes will perk up the living room, den, or a child's bedroom.

Rabbits, Raccoon, Squirrels and Deer

SIZE:

Each design area, 4″-5″ high.

EQUIPMENT:

Ruler. Straight pin. Basting thread. Tapestry needle. Embroidery hoop (optional). Steam iron.

MATERIALS:

For each picture: Charles Craft 11-count "Fiddler's Cloth," piece at least 8″ square; for mail order information, see Buyers' Guide, page 174. DMC six-strand embroidery floss, one skein each color listed in motif's color key. Wooden frame (ours are 6″ square). Mat board to fit frame.

DIRECTIONS:

Read Cross-Stitch How-To's, page 177; prepare fabric piece for embroidery. Baste across piece in both directions, to mark center point. Measure from center to mark starting point as follows:

Deer, $2\frac{1}{8}$″ up, $\frac{1}{2}$″ to the right.
Squirrels, $2\frac{3}{8}$″ up, $\frac{1}{2}$″ to the right.
Rabbits, $2\frac{1}{8}$″ up, $\frac{3}{8}$″ to the right.
Raccoon, $2\frac{1}{4}$″ up, $\frac{3}{8}$″ to the right.

Using three strands of floss in tapestry needle, work design in cross-stitch; make each stitch over one woven "square" of fabric. When cross-stitch is completed, work backstitches, following solid lines on charts and using two strands of dark brown floss. For rabbits, work straight-stitch whiskers, using one strand of dark brown floss. For squirrels, work French knot eyes at triangles on chart, using two strands of dark brown floss. For stitch details, see page 178.

Press completed embroidery on a well-padded surface. Mount and frame as desired.

DEER

- e Spring Green #471
- O Gray-Green #3052
- Medium Olive #469
- Dark Olive #935
- Forest Green #934
- = Light Taupe #842
- • Medium Taupe #840
- X Dark Taupe #839
- Deep Taupe #838
- Dark Brown #3371

SQUIRRELS

- Straw #3047
- Dark Tan #3045
- r Bright Gold #783
- c Dark Gold #781
- Ø Sage Green #3012
- Dark Olive #935
- Forest Green #934
- z Toast #435
- Light Chocolate Brown #433
- Dark Brown #3371
- = Light Taupe #842
- • Medium Taupe #840
- X Dark Taupe #839
- Deep Taupe #838

RABBITS
- Yellow #3078
- Gold #976
- Spring Green #471
- Medium Olive #469
- Dark Olive #935
- Forest Green #934
- Light Antique Rose #316
- Dark Antique Rose #315
- Toast #435
- Light Chocolate Brown #433
- Medium Chocolate Brown #801
- Dark Brown #3371
- Light Taupe #842
- Medium Taupe #840
- Dark Taupe #839

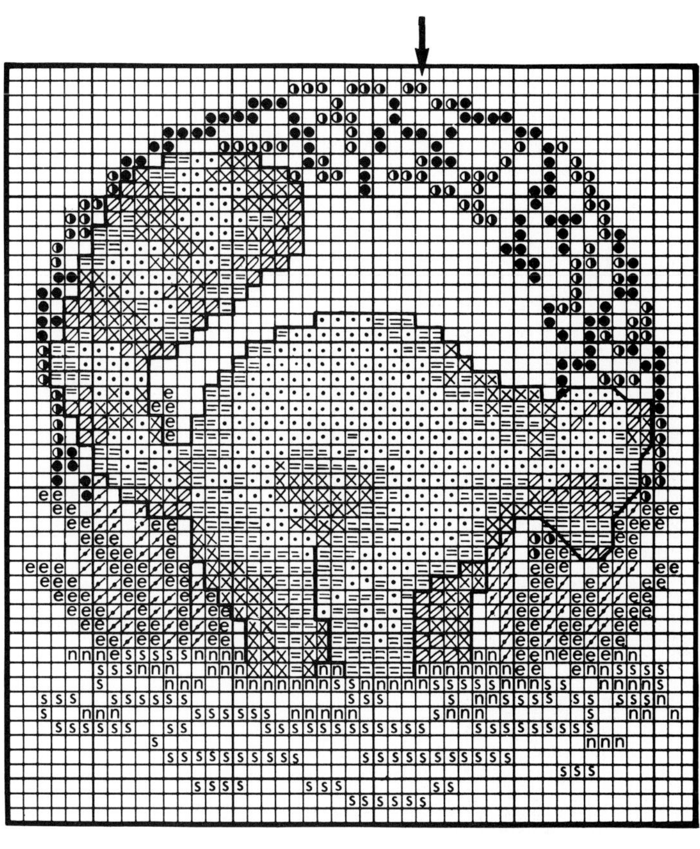

RACCOON
- Spring Green #471
- Medium Olive #469
- Dark Olive #935
- Forest Green #934
- Light Blue #3325
- Medium Blue #312
- Light Taupe #842
- Medium Taupe #840
- Dark Taupe #839
- Deep Taupe #838

Dark Brown #3371

Country accents...

Use cross-stitch floral designs to enhance many accessories in and out of your home.

opposite page: Nosegay Cabinet and Towels

Nosegay Cabinet and Towels

Floral patterns will brighten any room, even the bathroom! Stitch them on towels or as an insert for an old-fashioned medicine cabinet.

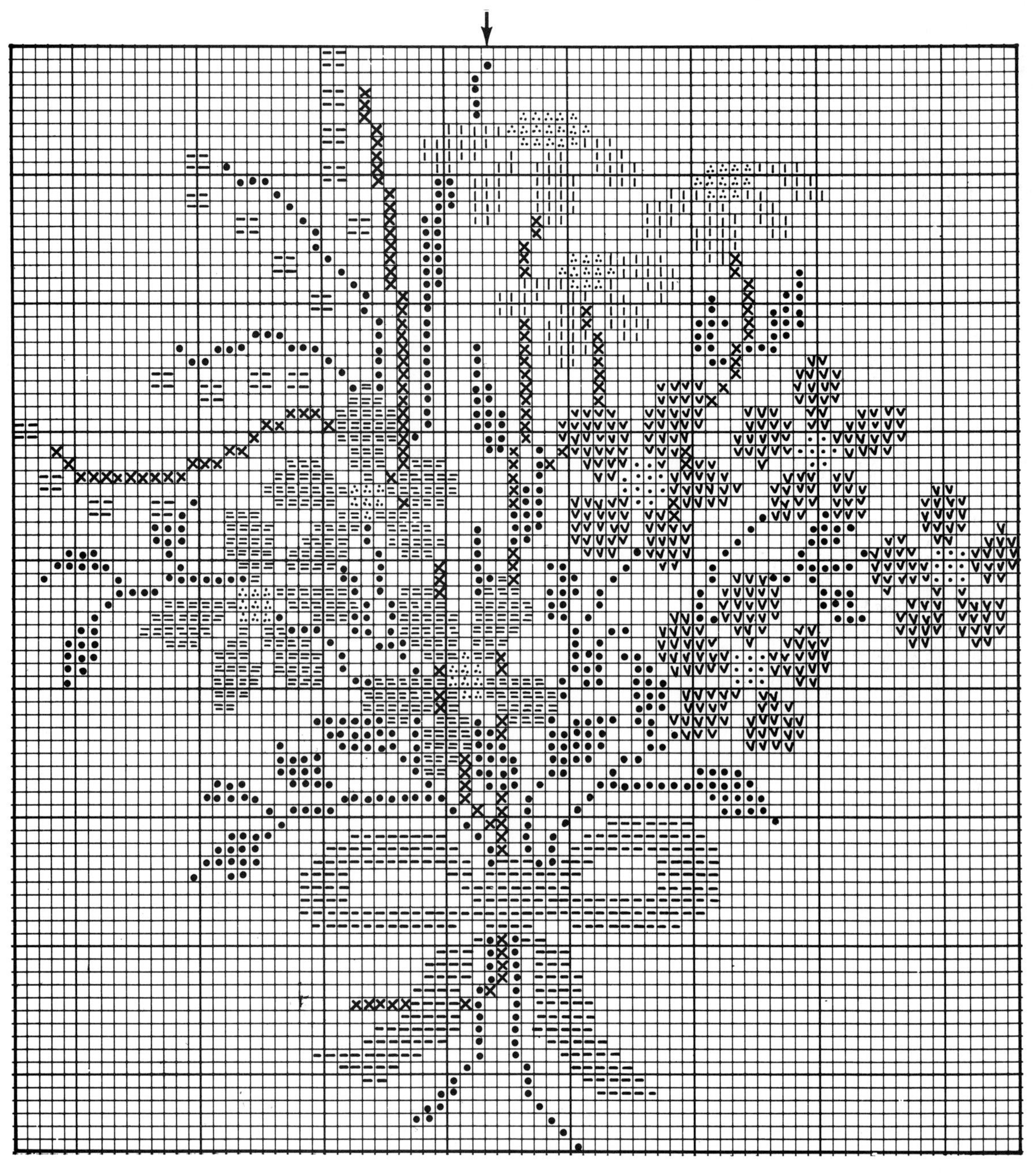

Nosegay Cabinet Insert

SIZE:

Fits a 7″ × 7″ opening.

EQUIPMENT:

Masking tape. Ruler. Straight pin. Embroidery hoop. Tapestry needle. Scissors. Steam iron. Pencil.

MATERIALS:

Ecru 14-count Aida fabric, piece 11″ square. DMC six-strand embroidery floss, one skein of each color listed in color key. Wheatland Craft's wooden medicine cabinet with 7″ × 7″ opening; for mail order information, see Buyers' Guide, page 174. Stiff cardboard, piece 8″ square. Batting, piece 8″ square. White craft glue. Brown paper (optional).

DIRECTIONS:

Read Cross-Stitch How-To's, page 177. Tape fabric edges to prevent raveling. Place fabric on work surface. Measure 2⅜″ down from top edge and 5⅜″ in from left edge; mark intersecting fabric threads, or "square", with a pin, for first stitch. Place fabric in embroidery hoop.

To work embroidery, follow chart and color key: Each square on chart represents one cross-stitch, worked over one square of fabric threads. Using two strands of floss in needle, stitch design, beginning at pin on fabric with stitch indicated by arrow on chart. When embroidery is completed, remove fabric from embroidery hoop. Steam-press piece gently on a padded surface.

Place cardboard against inside of cabinet door; tape in place temporarily. Working from front, use pencil to trace door opening onto cardboard. Remove cardboard from door. Draw a second line on cardboard, ¼″ outside traced line. Cut out cardboard along outer line. Test-fit into door opening. Trim cardboard until it fits loosely. Place cardboard octagon on batting; mark, then cut batting same size as cardboard. Glue batting to one side of cardboard, matching edges. Place embroidery face down on work surface. Center cardboard, batting side down, over embroidery. Fold fabric edges to back of cardboard and tape temporarily. Check to make sure design is centered on front, then glue fabric edges to cardboard, trimming fabric to prevent bumps. When dry, dot glue around inside of rabbet edge on door; place embroidery face out into opening; make sure design is positioned properly, then weight embroidery from back until glue is dry. If desired, cover back of door opening with brown paper, trimming paper ½″ larger all around than opening and gluing in place.

CABINET INSERT

- [●] Medium Green #989
- [X] Dark Green #319
- [=] Light Pink #3689
- [−] Dark Pink #718
- [I] Lavender #210
- [V] Cornflower #340
- [∴] Yellow #445
- [·] Orange #741

Nosegay Towels

SIZE:

Each design area, 3″ wide.

EQUIPMENT:

Tapestry needle. Basting thread. Scissors. Straight pin.

MATERIALS:

For each: Empress® cross-stitch towel from Charles Craft, 15″ × 26″; for mail order information, see Buyers' Guide, page 174. DMC six-strand embroidery floss, one skein of each color listed in color key.

DIRECTIONS:

Read Cross-Stitch How-To's, page 177. Baste center lines across cross-stitch area in both directions, to mark center of work. Following individual directions below, measure up from center along vertical line and mark position of first stitch with a pin.

To work cross-stitches, cut floss into 18″ lengths; separate strands and work with three strands in needle throughout. Following chart, start design at pin with stitch marked by arrow on chart. Each symbol on chart represents one cross-stitch worked over one "square" of fabric threads. When entire chart has been completed, repeat chart or work chart in reverse to complete design, as directed below.

Monogram: Measure up 1¼″ from center for first stitch of border. Complete chart, then continue border across towel. Turn chart upside down and work lower border in same way, beginning 1¼″ down from center. To work monogram, follow alphabet chart and work fuchsia initial at center of embroidered band. If desired, fill in open area of initial with lavender cross-stitches.

Hearts and Bows: Measure up 1⅝″ from center for first stitch. Complete chart, then continue design out to edges of towel.

Floral: Start at center for first stitch. Complete chart, then repeat design out to edges of towel, alternating petal colors as desired.

HEARTS AND BOWS TOWEL

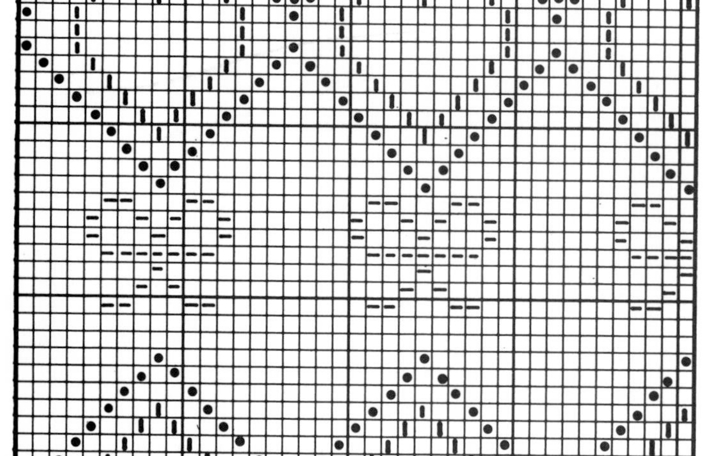

FLORAL TOWEL

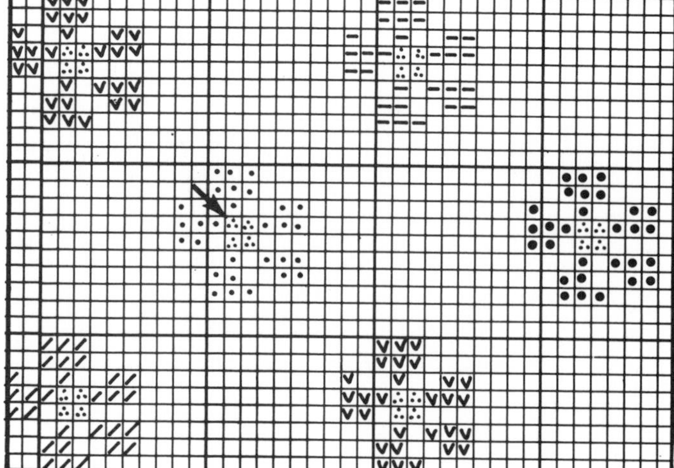

MONOGRAM TOWEL

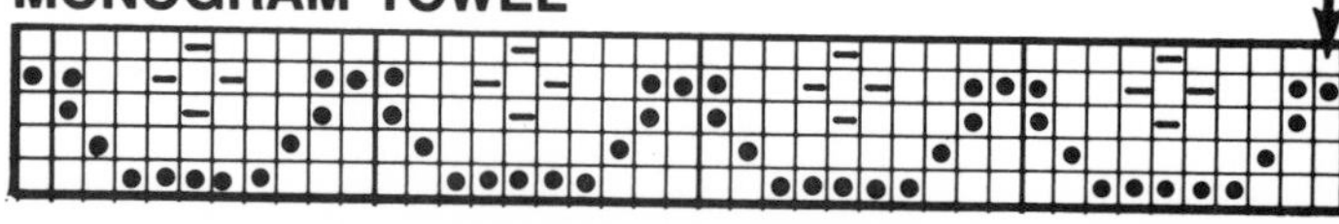

HEARTS AND BOWS TOWEL

- ■ Blue-Violet #340
- ■ Coral #3326
- ■ Rose #3687

FLORAL TOWEL

- ■ Lavender #554
- ■ Light Pink #3689
- ■ Coral #3326
- ■ Rose #3687
- ■ Blue-Violet #340
- ■ Fuchsia #718

MONOGRAM TOWEL

- ■ Fuchsia #718
- ■ Lavender #554

Floral Checkerboard Picnic

"Hopscotch" fabric makes an instant frame for the floral motifs on the pillows and runner of this picnic set.

Hopscotch Pillows

SIZE:

Each pillow, 14″ square, plus ruffle.

EQUIPMENT:

Masking tape. Ruler. Pencil. Scissors. Embroidery hoop. Tapestry needle. Straight pins. Sewing needle or sewing machine. Iron.

MATERIALS:

For each: Charles Craft 14-count Hopscotch fabric; green/white, red/white, or blue/white 15″-square pillow piece; for mail order information, see Buyers' Guide, page 174. DMC six-strand embroidery floss: one skein each of light pink #3354, burgundy #498, yellow #741, green #909 and blue #792 (enough for all three pillows). Unbleached muslin 48″ wide, ¾ yard (1½ yards will make all three). Ecru cluny lace 2″ wide, 5 yards. Pillow form, 14″ square. Ecru sewing thread.

DIRECTIONS:

Read Cross-Stitch How-To's, page 177. Tape fabric edges to prevent raveling. Fold fabric into quarters to find exact center and mark thread with a pin. Place fabric in embroidery hoop. Begin embroidery at center, following chart and color key. Work each design with two strands of floss in needle, making each cross-stitch over two "squares" each way of horizontal and vertical threads and counting two squares for each blank square on chart.

When embroidery is completed, remove fabric from hoop and remove tape from fabric edges. Pin lace around pillow front, straight edges even and with lace facing center of pillow front. Stitch in place making ½″ seam. For pillow back, cut a piece of muslin 15″

(continued)

RED/WHITE PILLOW

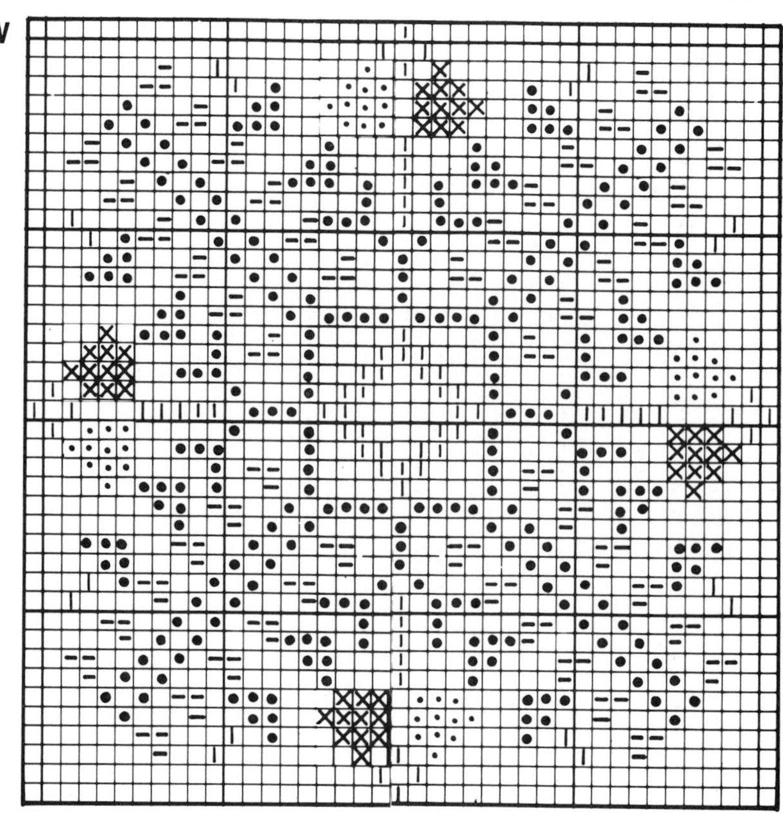

RED/WHITE PILLOW

- ⊡ Light Pink
- ● Burgundy
- ▬ Green
- Ⅰ Yellow
- ☒ Blue

square. To make ruffle, cut two strips from muslin, each 5½" × 42"; join with ½" seam to make a strip 5½" × 83". Join ends to make strip continuous. Fold strip in half lengthwise, right side out; press along fold. Work a row of running stitches (or long basting stitches on sewing machine) ¼" and ½" in from raw edge, sewing through both layers; pull ends of threads to gather strip to 60" long. Adjust gathers evenly and pin and baste ruffle to pillow front over lace, matching raw edges. Place pillow back on pillow front, right sides together and enclosing lace and ruffle. Sew all around with ½" seam, leaving a 6" opening for turning. Turn pillow cover right side out. Insert pillow form; fold raw edges of opening in ½" and slip-stitch opening closed.

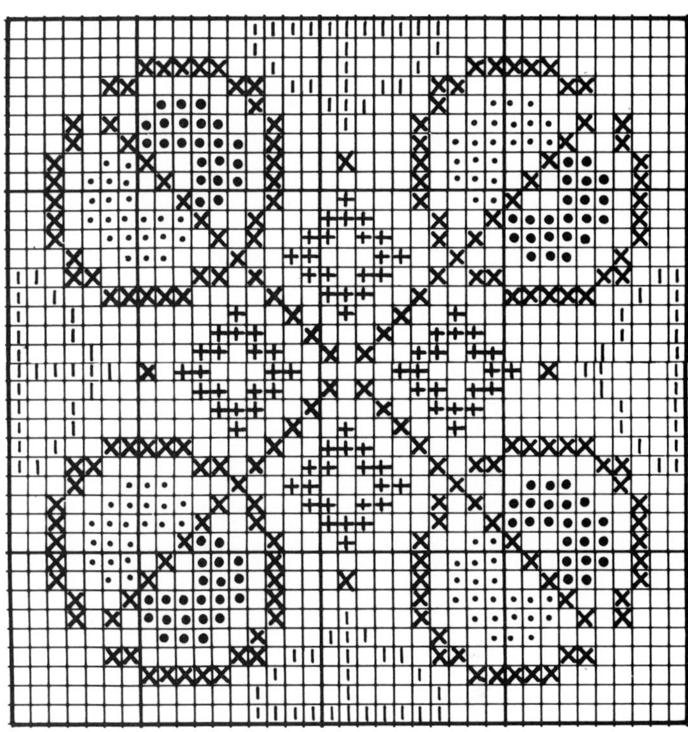

GREEN/WHITE PILLOW

GREEN/WHITE PILLOW

- ⊡ Light Pink
- ● Burgundy
- ☒ Green
- ⊟ Yellow
- ⊞ Blue

BLUE/WHITE PILLOW

BLUE/WHITE PILLOW

- ⊡ Light Pink
- ☒ Burgundy
- ◪ Green
- ⊟ Yellow
- ◫ Blue

Hopscotch Table Runner

SIZE:

14″ × 44½″, plus edging.

EQUIPMENT:

Masking tape. Embroidery scissors. Tapestry needle. Straight pins. Embroidery hoop. Sewing machine. Steam iron.

MATERIALS:

Charles Craft 14-count Hopscotch fabric, 15″ × 45½″ blue/white runner piece; for mail order information, see Buyers' Guide, page 174. DMC six-strand embroidery floss, two skeins blue #930. Ecru cluny lace 2″ wide, 3⅜ yards. Blue sewing thread.

DIRECTIONS:

Read Cross-Stitch How-To's, page 177. Tape fabric edges to prevent raveling. Fold each of the white squares into quarters to find exact center and mark each center thread with a pin. Place one square of fabric in hoop and begin embroidery at middle of center motif, following chart. Work design with two strands of floss in needle, making each cross-stitch over a "square" of one horizontal and one vertical fabric thread. Complete one motif in each of the three white squares.

After embroidery is completed, fold all four edges of fabric ½″ to back and press. Pin lace all around edges on back of runner, overlapping lace ends at one short edge. Topstitch lace to runner.

Colonial Sampler with Potted Chrysanthemums

Potted chrysanthemums and other folk motifs are combined for a traditional sampler, then used individually on many gifts and accessories.

Framed Sampler

SIZE:

Design area, 10″ × 12¾″.

EQUIPMENT:

Ruler. Masking tape. Straight pin. Embroidery hoop. Tapestry needle. Scissors. Iron.

MATERIALS:

White 22-count hardanger fabric, piece 18″ × 20″. DMC six-strand embroidery floss: one skein of each color listed in color key, unless otherwise indicated in parentheses. Frame with rabbet opening at least 12″ × 15″. Sturdy cardboard to fit frame.

DIRECTIONS:

Read Cross-Stitch How-To's, page 177. Prepare fabric as directed. Place fabric with longer edges at sides. Measure 4½″ down and 4″ in from top right corner; mark fabric thread with pin. Place fabric in hoop. Work sampler in cross-stitch, following chart and color key and beginning at pin with green stitch in upper right corner of trellis border. Use three strands of floss in needle and work each cross-stitch over a "square" of three horizontal and three vertical fabric threads. Work right half of design following chart, then reverse chart to work left half, omitting center vertical row of stitches indicated by star. (*Note:* Brackets and arrows on chart refer to other projects.) When charted design is completed, fill in upper corners with initials and date, following alphabet chart for characters and color photograph for placement.

When all embroidery is completed, remove fabric from hoop; press. Finish and mount piece, following directions in Embroidery Basics (see page 175). Frame sampler as desired.

SEC
1984
ABCDEFGH
JKLMNOP
STUVWXY
012345678

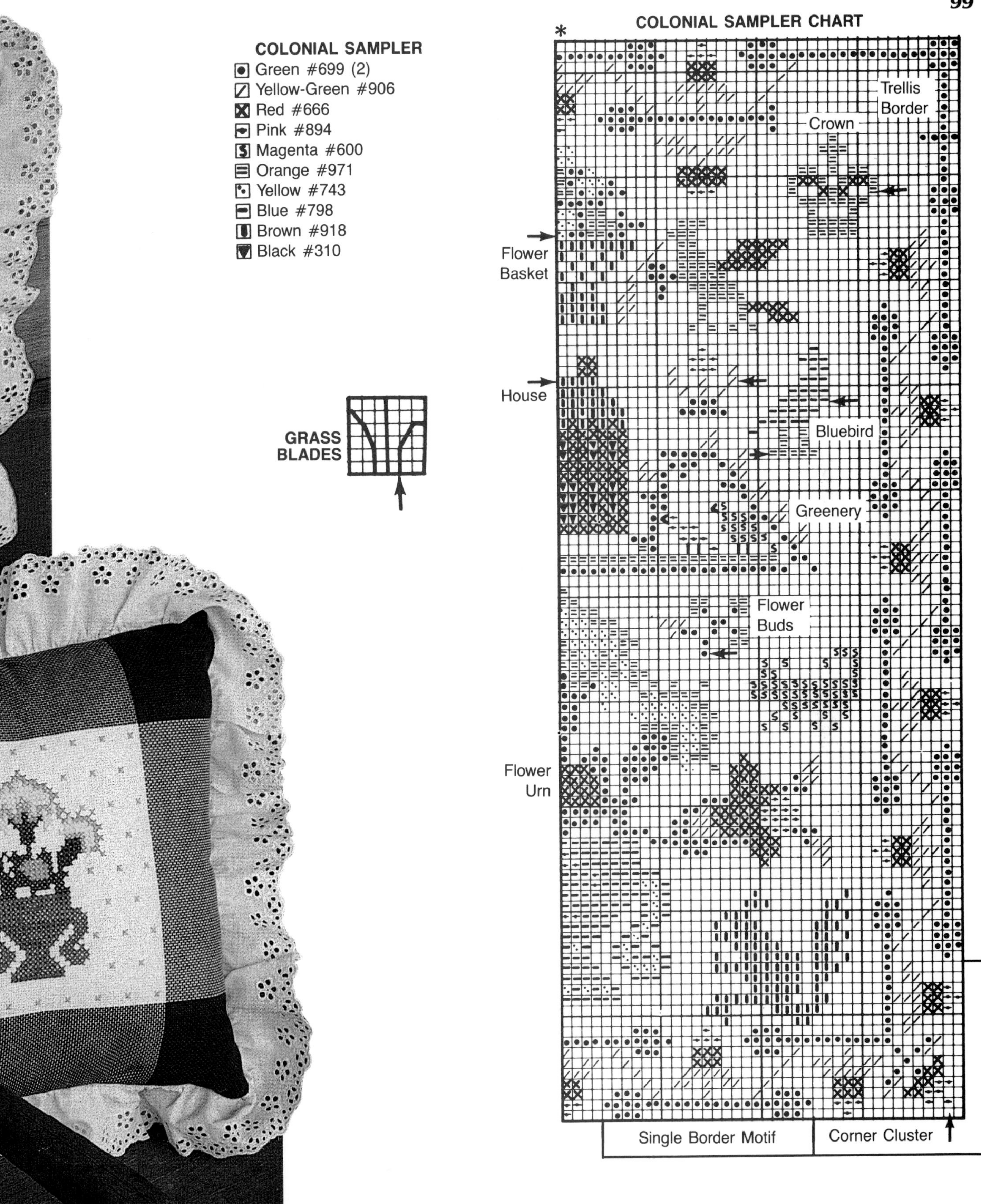
COLONIAL SAMPLER
Green #699 (2)
Yellow-Green #906
Red #666
Pink #894
Magenta #600
Orange #971
Yellow #743
Blue #798
Brown #918
Black #310
GRASS BLADES
COLONIAL SAMPLER CHART
Trellis Border
Crown
Flower Basket
House
Bluebird
Greenery
Flower Buds
Flower Urn
Single Border Motif
Corner Cluster

Sampler Pillow

SIZE:

12″ square, plus ruffle.

EQUIPMENT:

Ruler. Masking tape. Straight pins. Embroidery and regular scissors. Embroidery hoop. Tapestry needle. Sewing needle. Sewing machine. Iron.

MATERIALS:

Zweigart® ecru 6-count Herta fabric, piece 14″ square; to order from Hansi's Haus, see Buyers' Guide, page 174. DMC Floralia 3-ply Persian yarn: two skeins brown #7448; one skein each green #7346, yellow-green #7341, pink #7818, magenta #7600, red #7666, orange #7940, and black; to order from Craft Gallery, see Buyers' Guide, page 174. Burlap or other fabric for pillow back, piece 14″ square. Ecru sewing thread. Ecru pregathered eyelet trim 2¾″ wide, 1½ yards. Pillow form 12″ square, or fiberfill.

DIRECTIONS:

Read Cross-Stitch How-To's, page 177. Prepare Herta fabric as directed. Baste a line down vertical center of piece, stitching through a solid row of threads; measure for horizontal center and mark closest fabric thread with pin. Place fabric in hoop. Work design in cross-stitch, following Colonial Sampler chart and color key on page 99 to stitch house and garden motifs. Separate yarn and use two plies in tapestry needle; make each cross-stitch over one "square" of fabric threads. To begin, count four squares above center pin along basted line and work a brown cross-stitch for top center of roof, indicated on chart by arrow. Stitch entire right half of house, ground birds, and greenery, then work chart in reverse to stitch left half, omitting center vertical row of stitches indicated by star. (*Note:* Work bottom row of roof all in brown, not as charted.)

When house, ground birds, and greenery are completed, work a row of pink flowers below house, using motif between house and bluebird on chart: Return to vertical center line and count four squares below grass to work top pink stitch of flower. Follow chart to complete flower, using light green rather than dark green for bottom rows; stitch three more flowers on each side of first flower, skipping two squares between upper leaves of adjacent flowers.

Stitch alphabet above house and numbers below flowers (see color photograph), using brown yarn, following alphabet chart on page 106; work each line of characters from vertical center of fabric out to sides: To begin alphabet, count up 28 squares above roof along basted line, for first stitch of E, indicated by top arrow of chart. Work alphabet, leaving three rows between lines. To begin numbers, count down four squares below flowers, then one square to the right, for first stitch of number 5, indicated by bottom arrow.

When all embroidery is completed, remove fabric from hoop; remove tape from fabric edges; press. Pin eyelet all around embroidered pillow front so that eyelet rests on front of fabric and gathered edge is even with fabric edges; overlap eyelet ends at bottom of pillow front and pin eyelet in folds at each corner, to prevent catching ruffles in stitching later. Baste eyelet in place ¼″ from edges; leave pins at corners. Place fabric piece for pillow back on pillow front with right sides facing and edges even, enclosing ruffle. Stitch ½″ from edges all around, leaving an opening for turning. Turn pillow right side out. Remove all pins. Insert pillow form, or stuff with fiberfill. Turn raw edges ½″ to inside; slip-stitch opening closed.

Potted Chrysanthemum Pillow

SIZE:

14″ square, plus ruffle.

EQUIPMENT:

Masking tape. Straight pins. Embroidery hoop. Tapestry needle. Scissors. Sewing needle. Sewing machine. Iron.

MATERIALS:

Charles Craft green/ecru 14-count Hopscotch fabric, 15″-square pillow piece; for mail order information, see Buyers' Guide, page 174. DMC Floralia 3-ply Persian yarn: one skein each blue #7899, red #7666, orange #7940, yellow #7435, green #7346, and yellow-green #7341; to order from Craft Gallery, see Buyers' Guide, page 174. Muslin for pillow back, piece 15″ square. Off-white sewing thread. Off-white pregathered eyelet trim 3″ wide, 1¾ yards. Pillow form 14″ square, or fiberfill.

DIRECTIONS:

Read Cross-Stitch How-To's, page 177. Prepare Hopscotch fabric as directed. Fold Hopscotch fabric in half to find vertical center (there will be 52 threads to the right and left of center); mark fabric thread with pin. Count 12 threads down from pin; mark again for upper left corner of first stitch. Place fabric in hoop. Work flower urn in cross-stitch, following Colonial Sampler chart and color key on page 99. Separate yarn and use one ply in needle to work each cross-stitch over a "square" of two horizontal and two vertical fabric threads.

Begin with uppermost orange cross-stitch indicated by arrow on chart; work the three orange/yellow flowers, then work the small red center flower, using orange yarn instead of red. Do not stitch the two red/pink outer flowers or their stems. Work right half of design as shown on chart, then work chart in reverse, omitting center column marked by star, for left half. Work a few green cross-stitches to fill in left stem area as shown in color photograph. Work all vase details in red, instead of yellow as shown on chart.

To complete embroidery, work yellow-green cross-stitches over background of center panel as follows: Count four fabric threads in from left edge and down from top edge of center panel for top left corner of first stitch; work over two horizontal and two vertical fabric threads. Counting eleven fabric threads to the right, stitch second cross-stitch on same horizontal threads as first cross-stitch. Continue row across center panel until there are nine cross-stitches in first row. Count eleven fabric threads below first cross-stitch row, then work a cross-stitch, centering stitch between first two cross-stitches of first row. Stitch three cross-stitches on left half of second row same as first row, then skip over motif and work three stitches to match on right half of second row. Work a total of nine rows of yellow-green cross-stitches, alternating first and second rows and skipping over motif.

When embroidery is completed, remove fabric from hoop; press. Pin eyelet edging all around embroidered pillow front so that eyelet rests on front of fabric and gathered edge is even with fabric edges; overlap eyelet ends at bottom of pillow front and pin eyelet in folds at each corner, to prevent catching ruffles in stitching later. Baste eyelet in place ¼″ from edges; leave pins at corners. Place fabric piece for pillow back on pillow front with right sides facing and edges even, enclosing ruffle. Stitch ½″ from edges all around, leaving an opening for turning. Turn pillow right side out. Remove all pins. Insert pillow form, or stuff with fiberfill. Turn raw edges ½″ to inside; slip-stitch opening closed.

Ribband™ Bookmarks

SIZE:

Each, 1⅞″ × 7″, plus fringe.

EQUIPMENT:

Straight pins. Tapestry needle. Scissors. Iron.

MATERIALS:

For each bookmark: Ecru Maxi-Weave Ribband™ from The Finish Line, 1⅞″ wide; 8¼″ length with blue, red, or ecru edging.* DMC six-strand embroidery floss: one skein blue #978 plus scraps of brown #918 and yellow-green #906, for Bluebirds Bookmark; one skein each pink #894, yellow-green #906, and green #699, for Pink Flowers Bookmark; one skein orange #971, for Crowns Bookmark. Fusible interfacing.

*For mail order information, see Buyers' Guide, page 174.

GENERAL DIRECTIONS:

Read Cross-Stitch How-To's, page 177. Place Ribband with long edges at sides. Fold Ribband in half crosswise; place a pin at fold, to mark horizontal center. Work designs in cross-stitch, following Colonial Sampler chart and color key on page 99 to work motifs; see individual directions.

After motifs are completed, work a row of cross-stitches at top and bottom of bookmark as directed, stitching over each "square" of fabric threads as specified. Trim ends of bookmark to ½″ from cross-stitched rows; press. Pull out horizontal fabric threads to stitched border, forming fringe.

Cut a piece of interfacing to fit back of bookmark, excluding fringe. Fuse interfacing in place, following manufacturer's directions. If desired, slip-stitch a ribbon to back of bookmark, covering interfacing.

Bluebirds Bookmark: Read General Directions. Count nine fabric threads (or squares) in from right edge along horizontal center and mark with a pin for first blue stitch, indicated on chart by arrow at bird's chest. Using three strands of floss, work each cross-stitch over a "square" of two horizontal and two vertical fabric threads. When center bluebird is stitched, count 15 threads up from top stitch of bird's chest and make a brown stitch directly above blue stitch. Work top bird in reverse of center bird, with brown stitch just made being back edge of foot under tail; see arrow on chart. Repeat top bird at bottom, with same spacing as before.

When birds are completed, work backstitch blades of grass in front of each bird, using three strands of yellow-green floss and following grass chart (see stitch detail, page 178). Begin at arrow on chart, working between third and fourth threads from bird's feet. Follow chart for top and bottom birds; reverse chart for center bird. Finish, following General Directions; leave eight rows between motifs at top and bottom and cross-stitch rows, worked in blue.

Pink Flowers Bookmark: Read General Directions. Work rows of pink flowers, using motif between bluebird and house on chart: Work first yellow-green stitch over first fabric thread in from right edge along horizontal center, indicated on chart by arrow. Use two strands of floss to work each cross-stitch over a "square" of one horizontal and one vertical fabric thread. Complete first flower, then stitch second flower to the left,

(continued)

leaving two threads between flowers; use yellow-green for bottom two rows. Skip two threads to the left, then stitch third flower same as first flower. Begin next row of flowers at arrow as before, on the eleventh row below bottom of stitched row, but one thread to the left of first flower; use only yellow-green for stem. Complete row and make seven rows in all, alternating green stems and the starting point of rows, for slightly staggered effect. Finish, following General Directions; leave five rows between motifs at top and bottom and cross-stitch rows, worked in pink.

Crowns Bookmark: Read General Directions. Count six fabric threads in from right edge along horizontal center and mark with pin for first orange stitch, indicated on chart by arrow. Using three strands of orange floss, work each cross-stitch over a "square" of two horizontal and two vertical fabric threads. When crown is complete, work top crown 1¼″ above center crown; stitch bottom crown 1¼″ below. Finish, following General Directions; leave five rows between motifs at top and bottom and cross-stitch rows, worked in orange.

ALPHABET AND NUMBER CHART

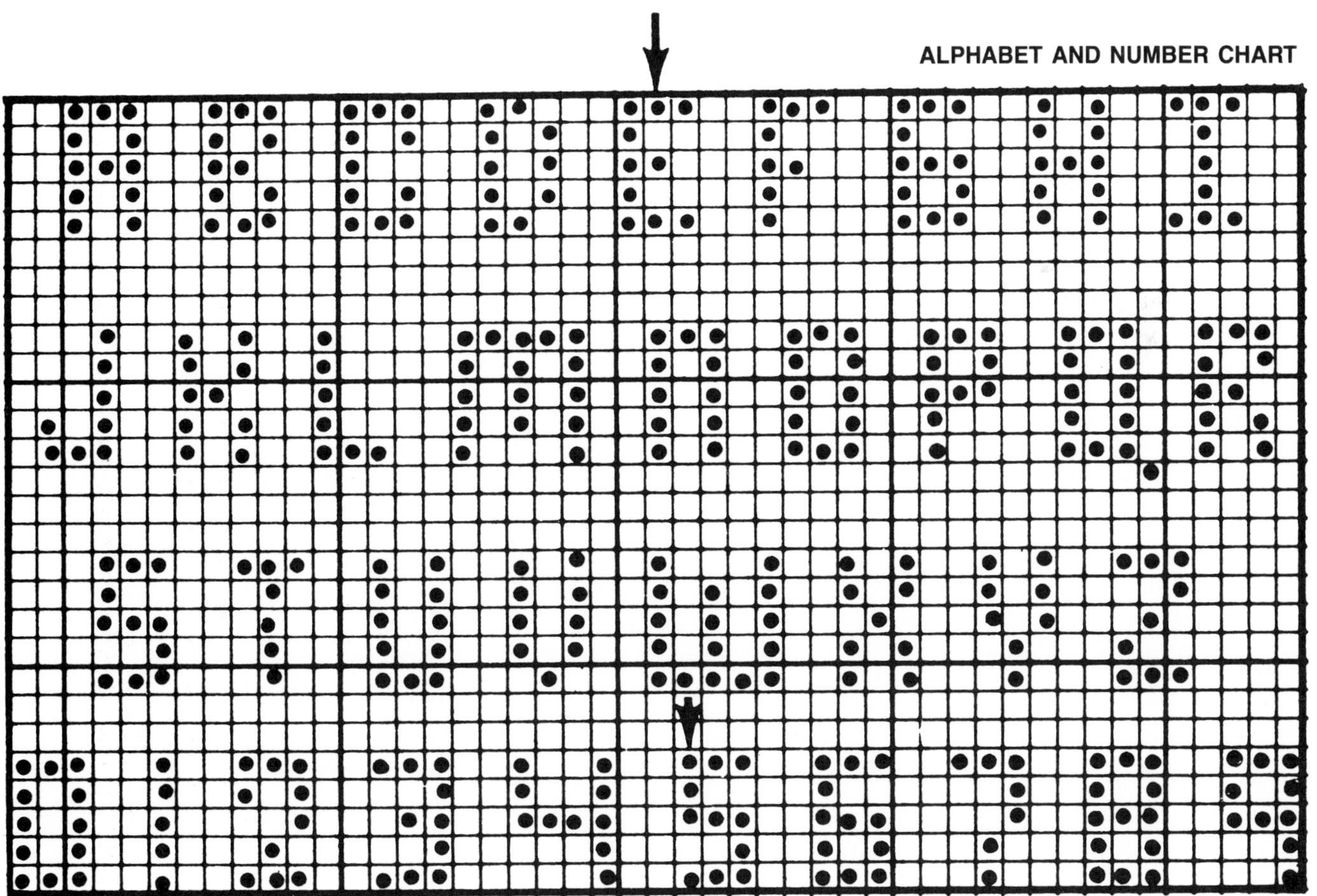

Trellis Place Mat and Napkin Ring Set

SIZES:
Place mat, 18½″ × 14½″; napkin ring, 1½″ wide.

EQUIPMENT:
Ruler. Masking tape. Straight pins. Embroidery hoop. Tapestry needle. Scissors. Sewing needle. Sewing machine. Iron. Water-erasable marking pen.

MATERIALS:
(for two mats and rings): Ecru 22-count hardanger fabric 43″ wide, ½ yard. DMC six-strand embroidery floss: two skeins green #699; one skein each yellow-green #906, red #666, and pink #894. Lightweight muslin 36″ wide, ½ yard. Ecru sewing thread. Fusible interfacing 22″ wide, ½ yard.

DIRECTIONS:
Read Cross-Stitch How-To's, page 177. Cut or mark hardanger fabric to size specified in individual directions below. Prepare fabric edges for embroidery. Determine placement of first stitch; mark fabric thread with pin. Place fabric in hoop. Stitch trellis border design in cross-stitch, following Colonial Sampler chart and color key on page 99, turning chart upside down to work motifs as directed; begin at pin with first stitch. Work each cross-stitch over a "square" of three horizontal and three vertical fabric threads.

When embroidery is completed, remove fabric from hoop; press, then cut as specified. Cut one piece each of muslin and interfacing the same size as embroidered piece. Fuse interfacing to back of piece, following manufacturer's directions. Place muslin on embroidered piece with right sides facing and edges even. Sew all around, leaving an opening for turning. Turn piece right side out. Turn raw edges to inside and slip-stitch opening closed. Press piece flat. For napkin ring, finish as directed.

Place Mat

Read Directions. Mark a 20″ × 16″ rectangle on hardanger; cut out on marked lines. Place piece with shorter edges at sides. Measure 1½″ down and 1½″ in from top left corner for upper left corner of first stitch; mark. Begin at pin with pink stitch in upper left corner of inverted chart, indicated by arrow. Stitch border design across long edge of fabric, repeating motif for seven pink flowers between corner clusters. Continue working down right side of fabric, placing five pink flowers between corner clusters. Work remaining two sides to match first two sides.

When embroidery is completed, trim fabric to 1″ beyond outermost green stitches. Finish as directed above, making ½″ seams.

Napkin Ring

Read Directions. Mark a 6½″ × 2″ rectangle on hardanger fabric; do not cut out until directed. Place fabric so that shorter edges of marked rectangle are at sides; mark vertical center. Measure ½″ down from top along vertical center; mark. Embroider single border motif, indicated by bracket; extend each green stripe at bottom to ¼″ from end.

When embroidery is completed, cut out piece on marked lines. Finish as directed above, making ¼″ seams. Fold piece into loop, butting ends; slip-stitch ends together.

Ribband™ *Basket Trim*

EQUIPMENT:

Ruler. Straight pin. Tapestry needle. Scissors. Iron.

MATERIALS:

Purchased basket. White Mini-Weave Ribband™ from The Finish Line, 7/8″ wide with pink scalloped edges, long enough to fit around basket top, plus 2″; for mail order information, see Buyers' Guide, page 174. DMC six-strand embroidery floss: one skein each of orange #971, yellow #743, yellow-green #906, and green #699. Double-faced masking tape 3/4″ wide.

DIRECTIONS:

Read Cross-Stitch How-To's, page 177. Place Ribband with ends at sides. Measure 3/4″ in from right end and count four threads up from lower scalloped edging; mark fabric thread with pin. Work flower buds in cross-stitch, following motif between house and flower urn on Colonial Sampler chart (page 99) and beginning at pin with green stitch indicated by arrow on chart. Use two strands of floss in needle and work each cross-stitch over a "square" of two horizontal and two vertical fabric threads. Complete first motif as shown, then measure 1 1/8″ to the left and mark with pin for second motif; work flowers in yellow, instead of orange. Continue to work motifs to within 1/2″ of left end of Ribband, alternating yellow and orange flowers.

When embroidery is completed, press band. Press ends 1/2″ to wrong side. Affix double-faced masking tape to back of Ribband so that raw ends are covered. Tape band around top of basket as shown in color photograph or as desired, overlapping ends. (*Note:* Masking tape can be removed easily for cleaning of embroidery.)

Flower Basket Coasters

SIZE:

3½″ diameter.

EQUIPMENT:

Pencil. Ruler. Masking tape. Straight pins. Embroidery hoop. Tapestry needle. Scissors. Iron. Compass. Thin, stiff cardboard.

MATERIALS:

For four coasters: White 22-count hardanger fabric, piece 8″ square. DMC six-strand embroidery floss: one skein each orange #971, yellow #743, brown #918, and green #699. One box of four tortoiseshell coasters for cross-stitch from Serendipity Designs; to order from Counted Thread, see Buyers' Guide, page 174. Fusible interfacing, piece 8″ square. Basting thread.

DIRECTIONS:

Read Cross-Stitch How-To's, page 177. Prepare fabric as directed. Fold fabric into quarters and baste along folds. In each 4″-square quarter of fabric, find center and mark fabric thread with pin. Place fabric in hoop. In each quarter, cross-stitch flower basket design, following Colonial Sampler chart and color key on page 99. Use three strands of floss in needle and work each cross-stitch over a "square" of three horizontal and three vertical fabric threads. To begin, place a yellow cross-stitch at threads marked by pin; this is lowest yellow stitch in design (indicated by arrow on chart) as well as center of design. Complete design in one quarter of fabric, then repeat in remaining quarters.

When all cross-stitching is completed, remove fabric from hoop; press. Fuse interfacing to back of embroidery, following manufacturer's directions. Use compass to draw a 2¾″-diameter circle on cardboard; mark center of circle. Cut out circle and push a pin through center at mark. For each coaster, place circle over one embroidered design, pushing pin through center yellow cross-stitch. Trace around edge of circle, using pencil. Cut out along pencil line; place in coaster, right side up. Insert clear top of coaster over embroidery.

Symbols of the Four Seasons

Preserve each season with cross-stitched pillows.

Four Seasons Pillows

SIZE:

Each pillow, 10″ square (plus ruffle).

EQUIPMENT:

Masking tape. Straight pins. Embroidery hoop. Tapestry and sewing needles. Ruler. Scissors. Steam iron. Sewing machine with zipper foot.

MATERIALS:

For each pillow: Zweigart® Monza fabric, piece 11″ square; to order from Hansi's Haus, see Buyers' Guide, page 174. DMC six-strand embroidery floss: one skein of each color listed in color key, unless otherwise indicated within parentheses; also, one skein gray #648 for summer pillow. Unbleached muslin, piece 11″ square. Fabric for backing and ruffle or boxing strip 55″ wide, ¾ yard. Sewing thread to match backing fabric. Fiberfill. **For ruffled pillow:** Ecru flat lace 2″-2½″ wide, 2 yards. Cotton cording ⅛″ wide, 1¼ yards. **For boxed pillow:** Cotton cording ⅜″ wide, 2½ yards.

DIRECTIONS:

Read Cross-Stitch How-To's, page 177. Tape Monza edges to prevent raveling. The center square on Monza cloth measures 31 × 31 fabric threads. To find center of center square, count 16 fabric threads down from the top and 16 threads in from either edge; mark intersecting fabric threads with a pin, for first stitch. Place Monza in embroidery hoop.

To work embroidery, follow desired charts and color key: Each symbol on charts represents one cross-stitch; heavy lines represent backstitches (see stitch detail, page 178). Work each cross-stitch over intersection of one horizontal and one vertical fabric thread, using three strands of floss in needle. Stitch center motif, starting at pin with center stitch indicated by arrows around charts. Using two strands of floss, work backstitches as directed below. Following border chart, stitch corner at upper left of fabric, then stitch center at top, aligning inner squares on chart with intersection of fabric threads for placement of corner embroidery and centering border center horizontally. For Spring pillow, continue gold bottom band to left edge of bracketed Border Center section. Work upper right corner, following chart in reverse. Turn fabric, then continue to work border centers and corners all around fabric. After all cross-stitches are completed, work backstitches as directed.

Spring Flower Basket: No backstitches are necessary.

Summer Strawberries: Work gray backstitches around white flowers, dark green backstitches for all stems and tendrils.

Autumn Leaves: Using all six strands of floss, work center leaf stem with dark coral backstitches. After all cross-stitches are completed, use two strands of floss to work dark orange leaf veins on the lighter half (left) of center leaf, dark coral leaf veins on the darker half (right) of center leaf, working over cross-stitches.

Winter Snowflakes: No backstitches are necessary.

Assembling: When all embroidery is completed, remove fabric from embroidery hoop; remove tape from fabric edges. Steam-press gently on a padded surface. Place muslin on back of embroidered pillow front, matching edges, then baste layers together along edges.

(continued)

For ruffled pillow: To make piping, cut a 1″-wide strip of backing fabric 45″ long. Center cording on wrong side of strip. Fold strip over cording so edges of strip meet; pin snugly against cording. Baste, remove pins, then machine-stitch as close to cording as possible, using zipper foot. Remove basting thread.

Pin piping around pillow front on right side so that raw edge of piping faces outward and seam is ½″ in from pillow front edges; overlap piping ends at a corner. Baste, then sew piping to pillow front. Remove basting thread.

Cut an 11″ square of backing fabric, then cut two 6″-wide strips, one each 30″ and 44″ long. Join ends with right sides facing and making ½″ seam, for a strip 73″ long. Fold strip in half lengthwise with wrong side in; fold strip ends ½″ to inside; press. Pin lace along strip with all raw edges even; sew ⅜″ in from raw edges. Machine-baste ¼″, then ½″ from raw edges; pull up bobbin thread and gather strip to about 42″ long. Pin ruffle around pillow front over piping with raw edges even; adjust gathers evenly. Sew ruffle in place just outside piping. Slip-stitch ends of ruffle together. Pin ruffle to pillow front so it won't get caught in seams. Place pillow back on pillow front with right sides facing and edges even. Sew all around ½″ from edges, leaving an opening along bottom for turning. Turn pillow right side out; remove pins. Stuff with fiberfill, fold raw edges in ½″, then slip-stitch opening closed.

For boxed pillow: To make piping, cut cording into two 45″ lengths. Cut two strips of backing fabric, each 2″ × 45″. Complete piping strips as for ruffled pillow. Pin one piping strip around pillow front as for ruffled pillow, except splice ends of piping together along one side as follows: Clip off excess piping, leaving 1″ extra on one end. On that end, clip seam open for 1″ from end; cut off 1″ end of cording. Turn under ¼″ of empty piping fabric and tack in place. On other piping end clip seam open for ½″ from end; cut off fabric, leaving ½″ of cording exposed. Insert exposed cording into empty piping fabric so that raw fabric end is covered; tack in place. Sew piping in place as for ruffled pillow.

Cut an 11″ square of backing fabric. Pin, then splice and sew second piping strip ½″ from edges as for pillow front. Cut a 3″-wide strip of remaining backing fabric the same length as measurement around piping plus 1″. Press each long edge ½″ to wrong side; unfold edges. Sew ends of strip together with right sides facing, making ½″ seam. Pin one long edge of strip around pillow front with right sides facing, so that fold line along strip edge is just outside piping. Baste strip in place, then remove pins. Sew strip in place along fold line. Pin and sew other edge of strip to pillow back in same manner, leaving an opening along one side for turning. Turn pillow right side out. Check to make sure all seams are properly sewn and fabric doesn't bunch anywhere; correct any problems. Stuff pillow firmly with fiberfill, turn raw edges in 2″, then slip-stitch opening closed.

BORDER CENTER

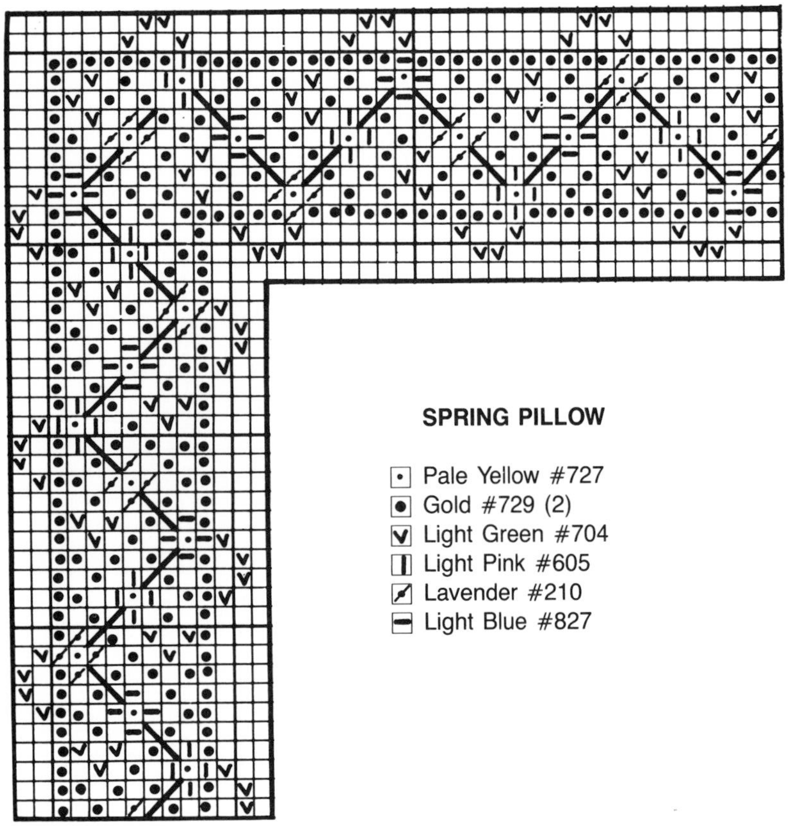

BORDER MOTIF

CENTER MOTIF

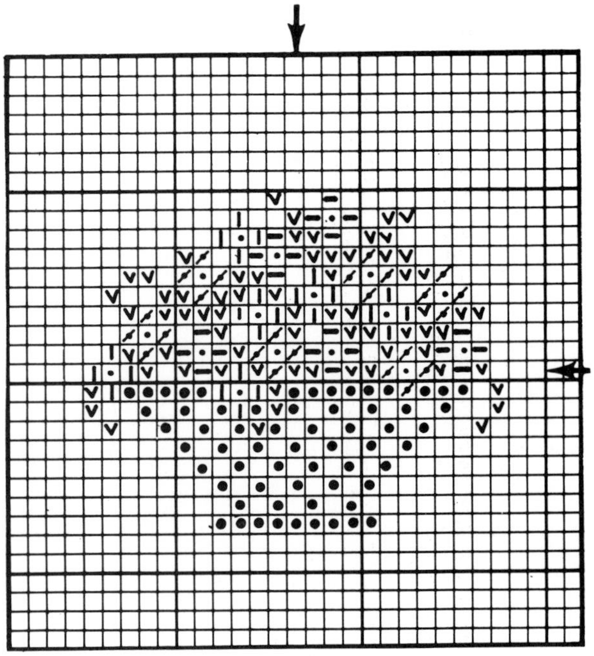

SPRING PILLOW

- Pale Yellow #727
- Gold #729 (2)
- Light Green #704
- Light Pink #605
- Lavender #210
- Light Blue #827

BORDER MOTIFS

CENTER MOTIF

SUMMER PILLOW

- Deep Red #321
- Dark Green #910
- White
- Medium Yellow #726
- Black #310

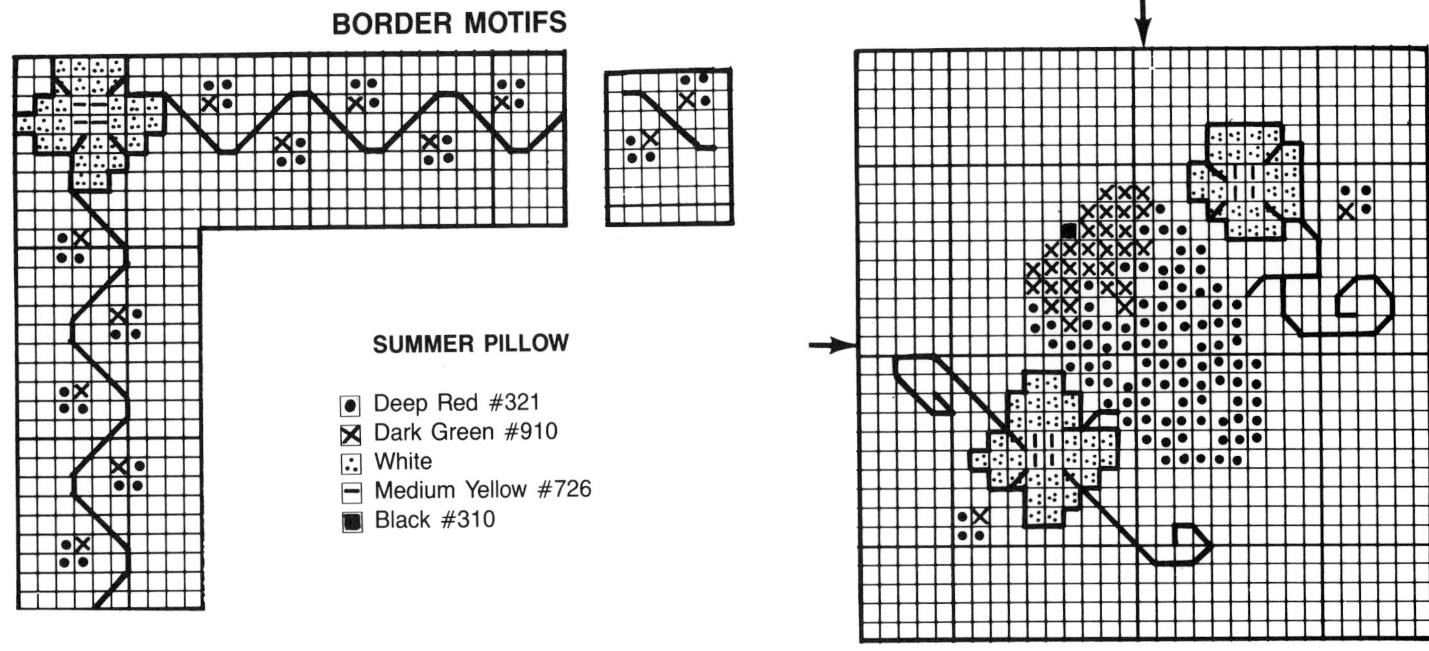

BORDER CENTER

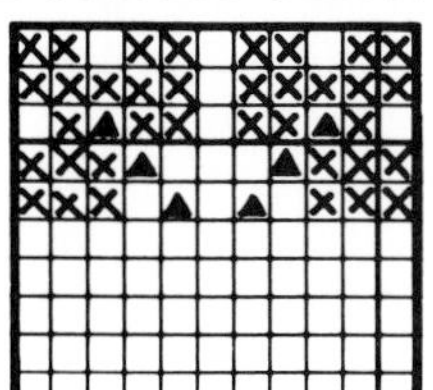

BORDER CORNER

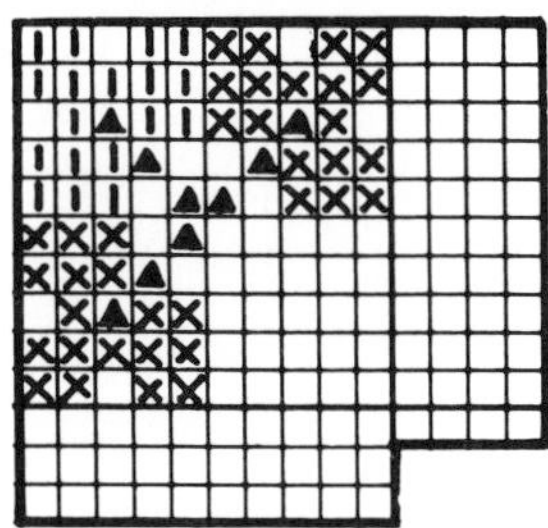

CENTER MOTIF

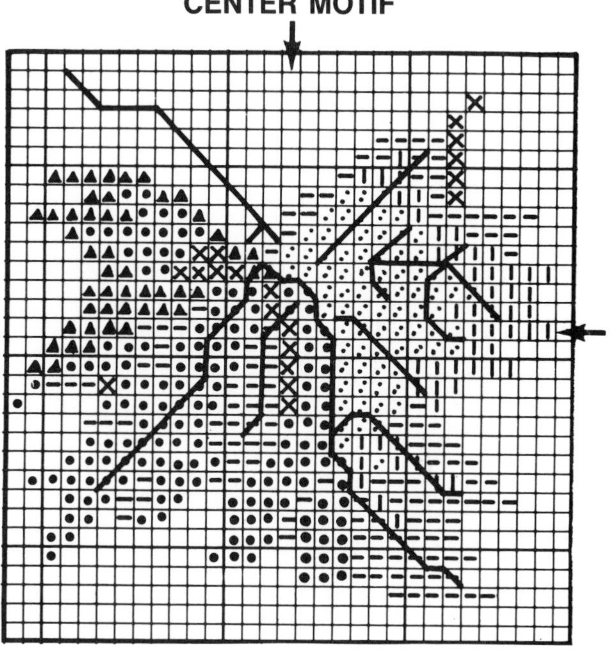

AUTUMN PILLOW

- ⊟ Light Orange #970
- ☒ Dark Orange #946
- ⊡ Medium Coral #3328
- ▲ Dark Coral #349
- ⁘ Medium Yellow #726
- ▯ Dark Yellow #972

BORDER CENTER

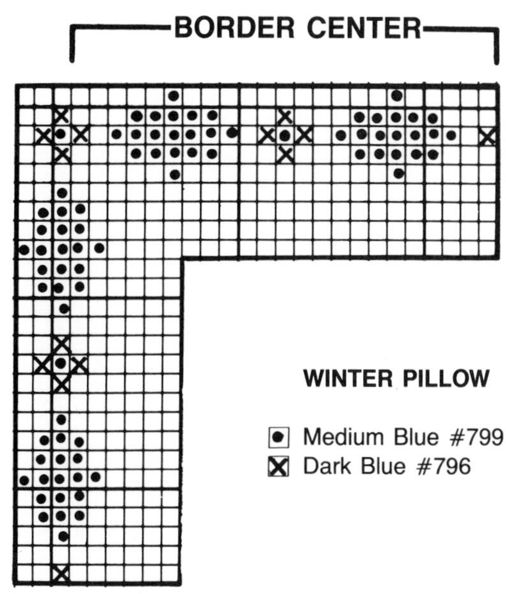

BORDER MOTIF

WINTER PILLOW

- ⊡ Medium Blue #799
- ☒ Dark Blue #796

CENTER MOTIF

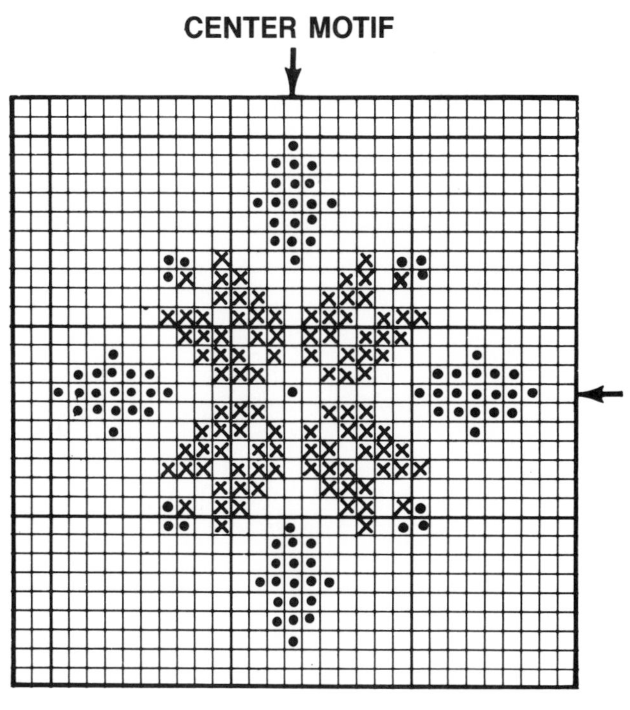

Flower-Banded Keepsakes

"Ribbons" of colorful flowers seem to bedeck a sachet, picture frame, pillow, and key case, but look again—the ribbon-stripes are actually cross-stitch!

Keepsake Picture Frame

SIZE:
Approximately 6½″ × 8¼″.

EQUIPMENT:
Pencil. Ruler. Scissors. Straight pin. Embroidery hoop. Tapestry and sewing needles. Mat knife. Sewing machine.

MATERIALS:
White 11-count Aida fabric, piece 8½″ × 10¼″. Six-strand embroidery floss, one 8-yard skein each color listed in color key. Masking tape. Batting. White craft glue. Scrap of white cotton fabric. Thin, stiff, colored cardboard. Pregathered lace ½″ wide in variegated pastels. White and dark-colored sewing thread.

DIRECTIONS:
Read Cross-Stitch How-To's, page 177. Prepare fabric as directed. With short edges of fabric at top and bottom, measure 1″ down and 1″ in from upper left corner for placement of first stitch; mark thread with a pin. Place fabric in hoop. Work design, following chart and color key and beginning at stitch marked by arrow. Separate floss and use two strands of floss in needle throughout. Work each cross-stitch over one horizontal and one vertical group of threads or one "square" of fabric. Work entire chart for upper half of frame. Turn chart upside-down and work lower half, omitting starred rows. After all embroidery is completed, remove fabric from hoop.

Using dark thread in sewing needle, baste along inside edge of embroidered frame. Measure inner and outer dimensions of embroidered frame; mark

(continued)

a frame on cardboard with same dimensions. Carefully cut out cardboard frame with mat knife; use as pattern to cut matching piece of batting. Glue batting to cardboard. Cut 5½″ × 7″ piece white fabric for facing. With right sides together, and facing centered over embroidered piece, stitch close to basting line; remove basting. Cut away both layers of center rectangle to within ¼″ of stitching line; snip into corners. Turn fabrics to right side; press. Pull facing through cardboard opening, with embroidered fabric on batting side and clipped seam allowance on cardboard side; seam should line up with inner edge of cardboard frame. Fold all edges to back of frame and glue in place, mitering corners. Using white thread, slip-stitch lace to back of outside edge of frame as shown.

For back, mark rectangle on cardboard same size as front; cut out. Cut three 1″-wide spacer strips from cardboard, two 8″ long for sides and one 4½″ long for bottom. Glue strips to back of frame; let dry. Spread glue on strips; press front and back frame pieces together, matching edges.

Following diagram, cut easel stand from cardboard. Using mat knife, score (do not cut through) stand along dash line for spine; fold along scoring, so that scoring is outside; spread glue on spine. Position spine, glued side down, on frame back, so that bottom edge of stand is flush with center bottom edge of frame; let dry.

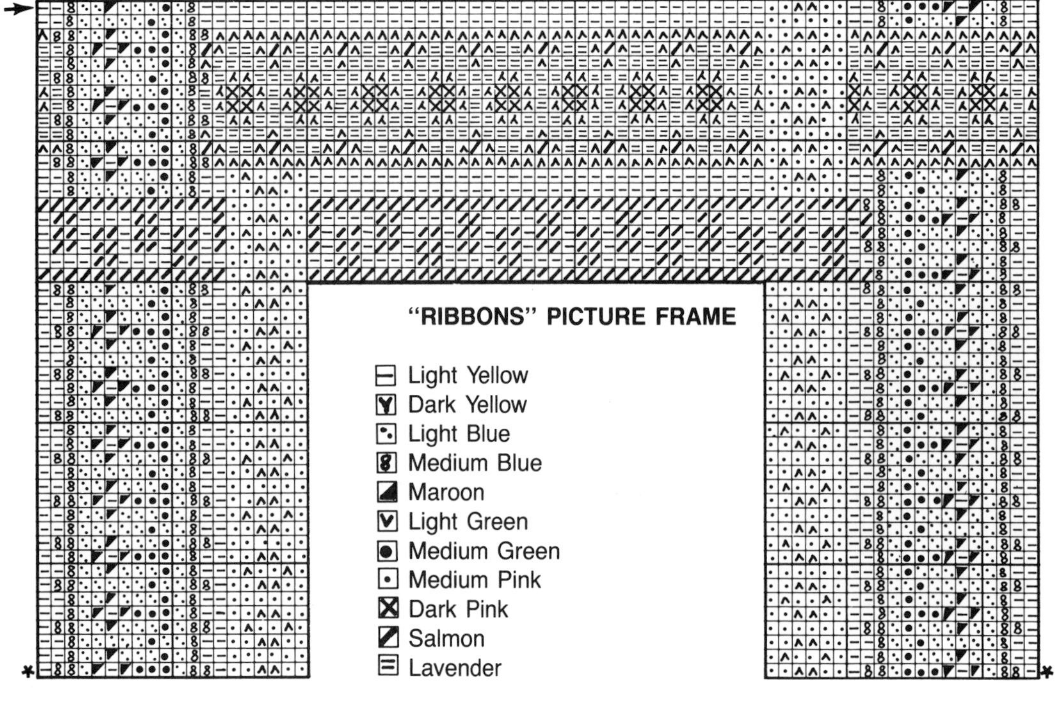

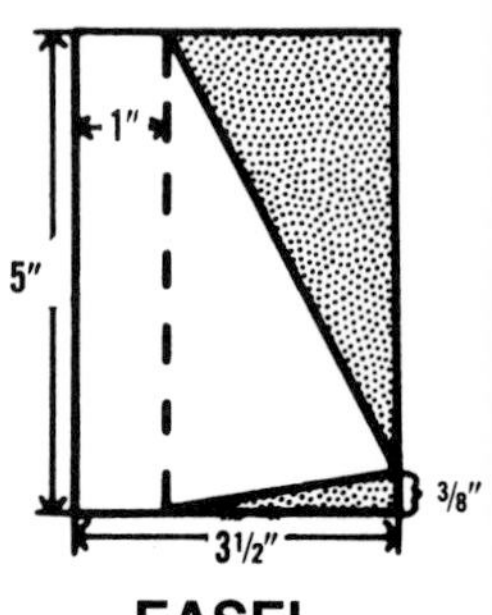

EASEL STAND

Keepsake Key Case

Shown on page 113

SIZE:
Approximately 2½″ × 4¼″.

EQUIPMENT:
Scissors. Straight pins. Tapestry and sewing needles.

MATERIALS:
White 11-count Aida fabric, piece 6″ × 7″. Six-strand embroidery floss, one 8-yard skein each color listed in color key. Scrap of felt for lining. Green 8″ non-separating zipper. Gold key ring, 1″ wide.

DIRECTIONS:
Read Cross-Stitch How-To's, page 177. Prepare fabric as directed. With short edges of cloth at top and bottom, measure 2″ down and 2″ in from upper left corner for placement of first stitch, indicated on chart by arrow; mark thread with a pin. Work design in cross-stitch, beginning at pin and following chart and color key. Separating floss, use two strands of floss in needle throughout. Work each cross-stitch over one horizontal and one vertical group of threads or "square" of fabric. Work entire chart, omitting starred row, for one side of case. Work chart again for other side, this time working starred row. When embroidery is completed, trim excess fabric around design to ½″; press to wrong side. Open zipper and spread sides apart, so that opening forms a ring with zipper ends and selvages inside. With right side up, place embroidery over zipper and align zipper ends with center row of center green band. Pin edges of embroidery to zipper selvages, so that embroidery overlaps zipper 1⁄16″ and covers ends; slip-stitch all around. Turn case over. Cut a 3¾″ × 5″ piece felt for lining and pin to wrong side, overlapping and concealing zipper selvages and ends; slip-stitch all around. Zip case closed. Attach key ring to zipper pull.

"RIBBONS" KEY CASE CHART

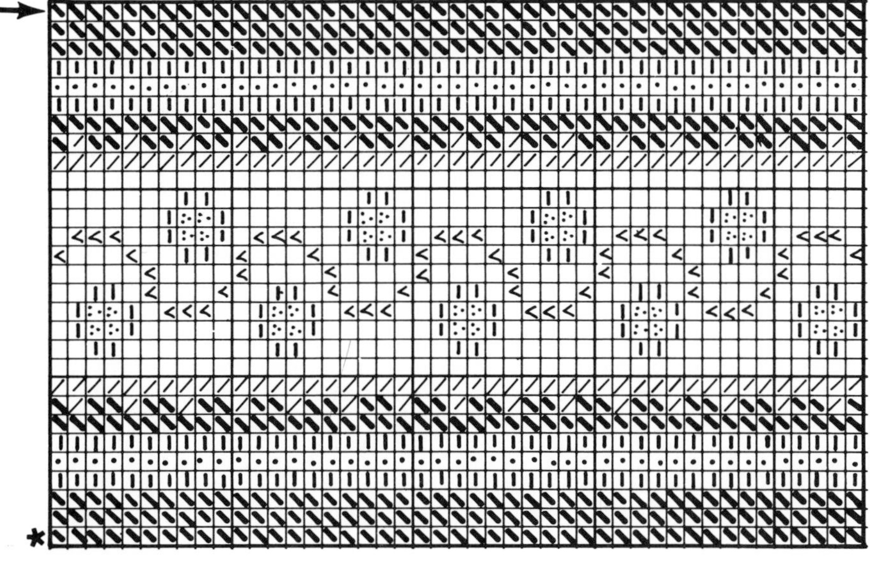

KEY CASE

- Yellow
- White
- Yellow-Green
- Green
- Rose
- Pink

Keepsake Pillow

Shown on page 113

SIZE:

11¼″ square.

EQUIPMENT:

Pencil. Ruler. Scissors. Straight pin. Embroidery hoop. Tapestry and sewing needles.

MATERIALS:

White 11-count Aida fabric, 13¼″ square. Six-strand embroidery floss, one 8-yard skein each color listed in color key. Masking tape. Fiberfill. White pre-gathered eyelet lace 1″ wide, 1½ yards. Cotton velvet, 12¼″ square for pillow back. White and dark-colored sewing thread.

DIRECTIONS:

Read Cross-Stitch How-To's, page 177. Measure 1″ down and 1¼″ in from upper left-hand corner of piece for placement of first stitch; mark thread with a pin. Place fabric in hoop. Work design, following chart and color key and beginning at stitch marked by arrow. Work each cross-stitch over one horizontal and one vertical group of threads or one "square" of fabric. Separate floss and use three strands of floss in needle throughout. After embroidery is completed, remove fabric from hoop. Using dark thread in sewing needle, mark edges of pillow front by basting along ends of "ribbons," following solid outline on chart. Measure basting and cut eyelet to fit, plus 2″. With right sides facing, pin eyelet to pillow edge so that top of eyelet overlaps basting line ⅛″. Fold ends under ¼″ and overlap where they meet; baste eyelet to pillow edge. With right sides facing, place velvet back, centered, over pillow front; pin. Stitch pieces together along basting line, leaving 2″ opening for turning; remove basting; trim seam allowance to ½″. Turn, stuff pillow with fiberfill; slip-stitch opening closed.

Keepsake Sachet

Shown on page 112

SIZE:

8¾″ square.

EQUIPMENT:

Ruler. Scissors. Straight pins. Masking tape. Embroidery hoop. Tapestry and sewing needles. Water-erasable pen. Sewing machine.

MATERIALS:

White 11-count Aida fabric, 11″ square. Ecru velvet or velveteen for backing, 11″ square. Ecru lace ¾″ wide, one yard. Six-strand embroidery floss, one 8-yard skein each color listed in color key. Beige grosgrain ribbon ⅜″ wide, ¾ yard. Sewing thread to match fabrics. Potpourri for stuffing.

DIRECTIONS:

Read Cross-Stitch How-To's, page 177. Prepare Aida as directed. Before working cross-stitches, divide cloth into boxes and strips for "log cabin" design following diagram; each square on diagram represents one group of threads or "square" of cloth: To begin, find center square by folding piece in half twice; mark center square with a pin. Beginning at pin (black square on diagram) and working outward from center in each direction, count off five squares for box A, which is 11 × 11 squares; mark corners with pin. Continue counting and

(continued)

PILLOW

- Light Yellow
- Lemon Yellow
- Dark Yellow
- Yellow-Orange
- Orange
- Yellow-Green
- Green
- Mint Green
- Olive Green
- Blue-Green
- Light Blue
- Medium Blue
- Turquoise
- Lavender
- Violet
- Purple
- Light Pink
- Dark Pink
- Red
- Salmon
- Peach
- Tan

PILLOW CHART

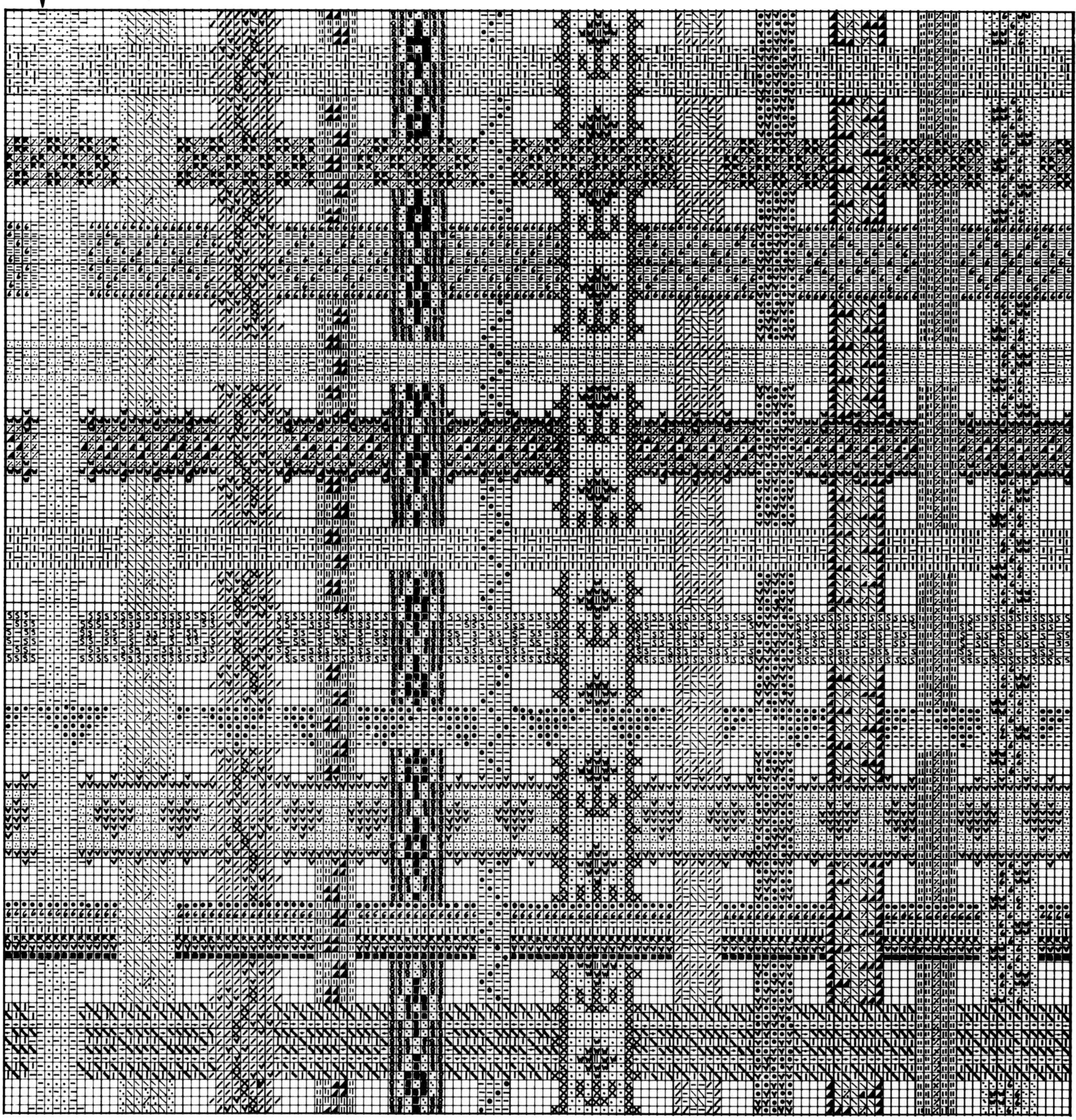

marking 11 squares for width of each box or strip; count squares on chart for length. Using ruler and water-erasable pen, mark strips on cloth, drawing lines between squares of fabric. Piece will be 99 × 99 squares. Place piece in embroidery hoop. Work cross-stitches, separating floss and using two strands in needle throughout; follow color key and chart corresponding to letter on diagram. To start, hold piece in same position as diagram. Begin at center box A and work one motif of chart A. Moving clockwise, turn piece 90 degrees and work box B, working one flower and two half flowers as shown in color photograph. Turn again and work strip B. Turn for long strip C, then for short strip C. Continue to turn piece and work strips in order until all have been worked.

Baste along inner and outer edges of the four outermost strips. On right side, pin lace so that straight edge overlaps outside basting 1/8" and curving edge faces center; ends should just meet. With right sides facing, place velvet backing and sachet front together; pin. Stitch pieces together close to outside basting, leaving 2" opening for turning; trim seam allowance to 1/2"; turn. Whip ends of lace together. On right side, topstitch close to inside basting line to form "pocket," leaving 3" unstitched, parallel to first opening. Stuff pocket with potpourri, then finish last 3" of topstitching; remove all basting. Turn edges at opening 1/2" to inside; slip-stitch opening closed. To make bows, cut four 6" pieces grosgrain ribbon. Cross ends to form mock bow; tack one bow to each corner of sachet as shown, wrapping thread around center of each.

SACHET CHARTS

A

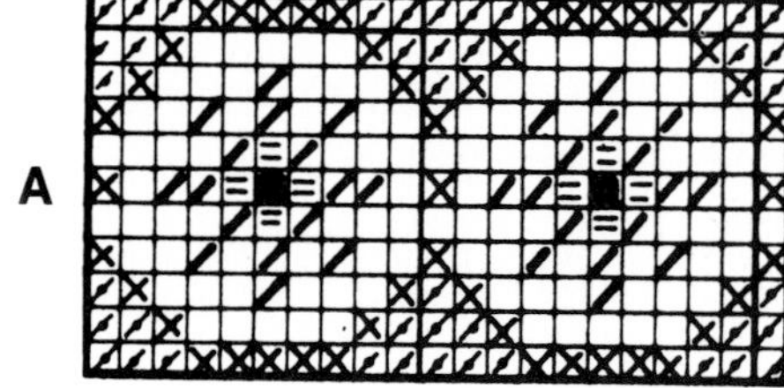

B

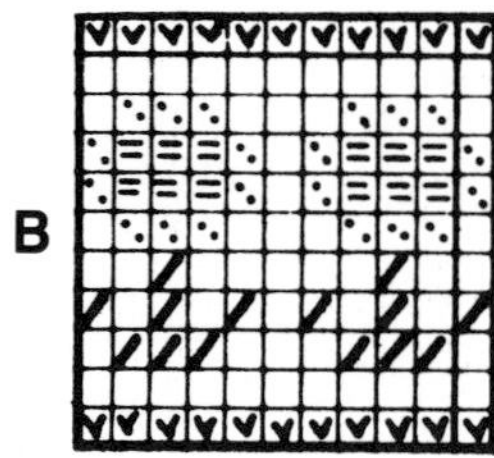

C

D

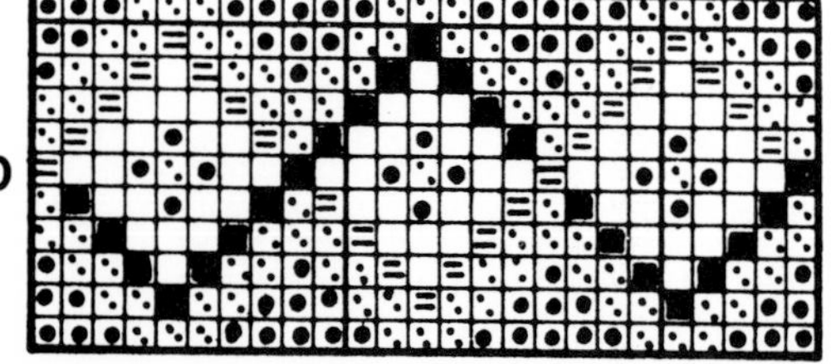

SACHET

- Olive Green
- Yellow-Green
- Rust
- Dark Brown
- Medium Brown
- Light Brown
- Navy
- Royal Blue
- Light Blue

SACHET DIAGRAM

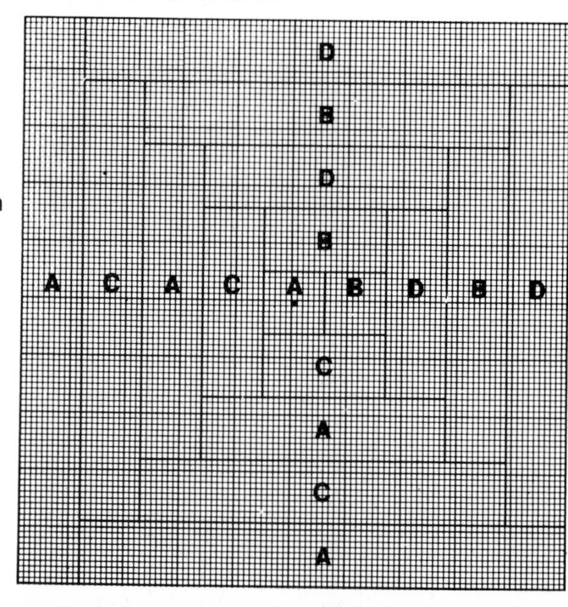

Strawberry Door Sign

Welcome friends with a cheery sign, bordered by strawberry vines.

Sign

SIZE:
$5\frac{1}{2}'' \times 7\frac{1}{2}''$.

EQUIPMENT:
Pencil. Ruler. Scissors. Tapestry and sewing needles. Dressmaker's tracing (carbon) paper. Paper for pattern. Dry ball-point pen. Iron. Embroidery hoop. Straight pin.

MATERIALS:
White 18-count Ainring fabric, piece 7" × 9". DMC pearl cotton size 8, one ball each of red #666, green #912, pink #894. Foamcore board, piece 5" × 7". Masking tape. Red twisted cord ¼" wide, 30". Red sewing thread.

DIRECTIONS:
Read Cross-Stitch How-To's, page 177. With short edges of fabric at sides, measure $2\frac{7}{8}''$ in and $2\frac{7}{8}''$ down from upper left corner for placement of first stitch, indicated on chart by arrow; mark intersecting fabric threads with pin. Insert fabric in hoop. Following chart, work saying in cross-stitch, using green pearl cotton in tapestry needle. Work each cross-stitch over one horizontal and one vertical group of threads or "square" of fabric. When cross-stitching is completed, remove fabric from hoop; set aside.

Draw lines across border pattern, connecting grid lines. Enlarge pattern by copying on paper ruled in 1" squares; cut out center. Place pattern face up over fabric with cross-stitched saying centered within border. Taking care not to move pattern again, place dressmaker's carbon between pattern and fabric and transfer pattern, using dry ball-point pen.

To embroider border, place fabric in hoop. Work lines of border in outline stitch (see stitch details, page 178), using green pearl cotton for stems, leaves, and strawberry tops, pink for petals, and red for flower centers and strawberries. Work dots in red French knots.

When embroidery is completed, remove fabric from hoop and steam-press lightly. Place embroidery face down on flat work surface. Center foamcore board on fabric. Fold fabric edges to back of board and tape in place. Cut 5" length from twisted cord; set aside. Slip-stitch remaining cord around edges as shown in color photograph. Tape ends of 5" cord to center back of board, leaving loop extending at top.

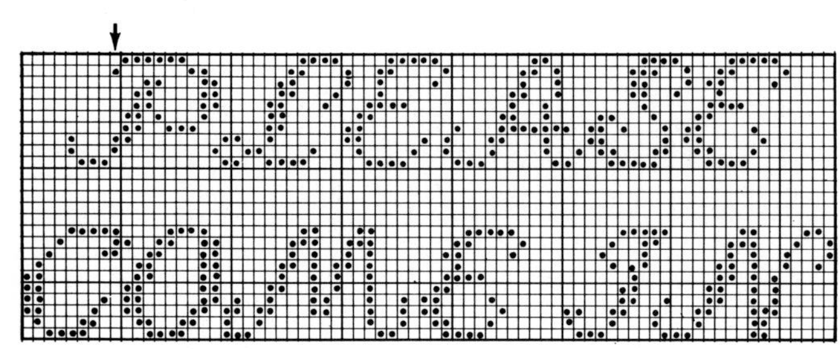

Oriental Poppies for a Boudoir

Unique cross-stitch fabric frames a pair of oriental poppies on this cord-edged pillow.

Poppies Pillow

SIZE:

9″ square, plus trim.

EQUIPMENT:

Ruler. Masking tape (optional). Water-erasable marking pen. Cotton swabs. Straight pins. Scissors. Sewing and tapestry needles. Embroidery hoop (optional). Sewing machine. Iron.

MATERIALS:

Zweigart® white "Shenandoah" fabric, with blue grid, two 12″ squares; to order from Hansi's Haus, see Buyers' Guide, page 174. Susan Bates Anchor® embroidery floss, one skein each color in color key, unless otherwise indicated in parentheses. Medium-blue pearl cotton size 5, one skein. White sewing thread. Fiberfill.

DIRECTIONS:

Embroidery: To prevent fabric from raveling, bind all raw edges of one fabric square (pillow front) with masking tape, whipstitch edges by hand, or machine-stitch ⅛″ in from edges. Locate center of prepared fabric; mark with straight pin. Count 16 threads up and six threads to the right of center; mark with pin for placement of first stitch.

Read Cross-Stitch How-To's, page 177. Work design in cross-stitch, following chart and color key and beginning with stitch indicated by arrow. Separate floss and work with three strands in embroidery needle. Each symbol on chart represents one cross-stitch worked over a "square" of two horizontal and vertical fabric threads. Different symbols and numbers represent different colors (see key). When moving from one area of design to another, be sure to count two fabric threads for each square on chart.

When all cross-stitching is complete, work additional embroidery with two strands floss in needle, following heavy solid lines on chart; for stitch details, see page 178. Outline center flower petals in backstitch, using dark blue floss for blue flowers and medium pink for pink flower. Work remaining flower details in straight stitch, using dark blue for blue flowers and red for pink flower. Work tendrils in backstitch, using dark green.

After backstitching is complete, remove fabric from hoop, if using one, and press gently face down on a padded surface.

Assembly: Cut away excess fabric margins, leaving two 10″ squares. Stitch pillow front and back together, wrong sides out, making ½″ seams; leave an opening for turning. Turn pillow to right side; stuff until plump. Turn raw pillow edges ½″ to inside; slip-stitch opening closed. Using pearl cotton, make a twisted cord to fit around pillow edges (see How to Make a Twisted Cord, page 179). Tack cord in place with invisible stitches.

ORIENTAL POPPIES BOUDOIR PILLOW

1 Light Pink #048
2 Medium Pink #031
3 Dark Pink #042
★ Red #038
4 Light Blue #0144
5 Medium Blue #0130 (3)
/ Dark Blue #0147
• Light Green #0214
● Dark Green #0210

Butterfly Tablecloth

Dainty butterflies flutter on this elegant damask tablecloth that has even-weave circles woven right in. Motifs can also enhance many small projects.

Butterfly Tablecloth

SIZE:

86″ × 64″.

MATERIALS:

Zweigart® "Stratford" damask, article 2188, 67″ wide, 2½ yards;* to order from Hansi's Haus, see Buyers' Guide, page 174. DMC six-strand embroidery floss: see key for colors (number of skeins needed of each in parentheses). Sewing thread to match damask.

***Note:** make sure fabric shows eight medallions for embroidery along length of goods. Finished cloth will measure eight medallions long × six medallions across.

DIRECTIONS:

To Prepare Damask for Embroidery: Place fabric on a flat surface with selvage facing you. Using pattern in damask as a guide, mark a point on selvage centered between two medallions so that there are four medallions on either side. From this point, measure 44″ to right and to left and mark with pins; make sure damask pattern is symmetrical on each side and adjust pins as necessary. When satisfied, pull thread across fabric at each end for crosswise grain. Cut across fabric along pulled threads and trim selvages ½″. Fold edges ½″ twice to wrong side, mitering corners if desired. Stitch by hand or machine.

On even-weave portion of each medallion, there are rows of 11 fabric squares each along top, bottom, and side edges. Baste from sixth (center) squares down and across; basting thread will intersect at center of medallion.

To Embroider Butterflies: Read Cross-Stitch How-To's, page 177. Tablecloth has 48 butterflies—24 yellow and 24 violet. To begin, follow arrows down and across each butterfly chart and, using a colored pencil, circle square where they intersect for first stitch. For each butterfly, follow chart and color key and begin at center of medallion with circled square on chart. Work butterfly in cross-stitch using three strands floss in needle; work antennae in backstitch using two strands floss in needle; for stitch detail, see page 178. Follow diagram for color and placement of butterflies in the medallions; arrowheads indicate direction of antennae.

When embroidery is completed, remove basting threads and steam-press cloth gently on wrong side on a flat surface.

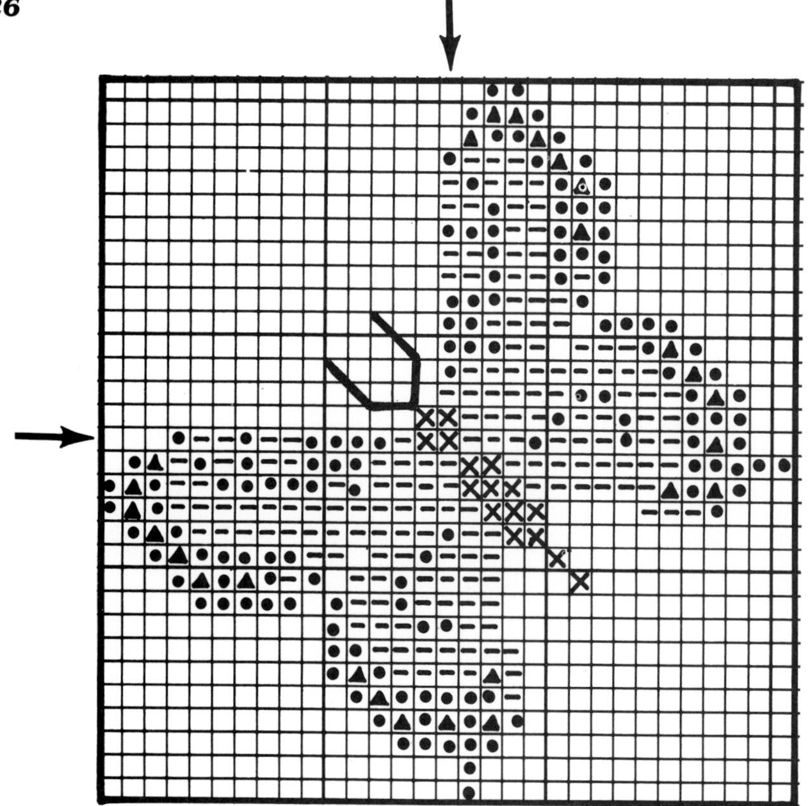

VIOLET BUTTERFLY
- Lilac #3609 (3)
- Amethyst #3607 (3)
- Violet #553 (2)
- Light Brown #435 (2)

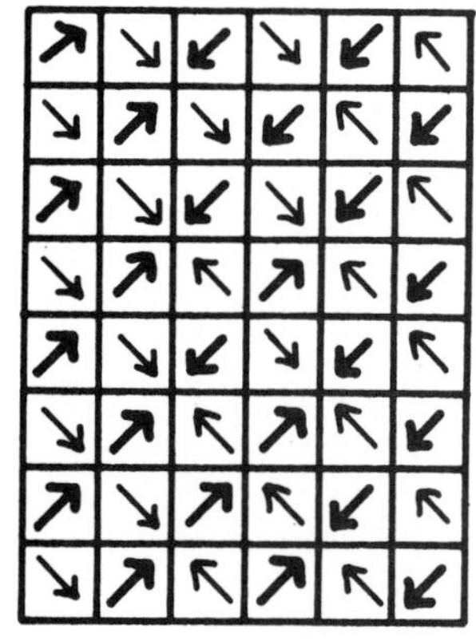

Violet
Yellow

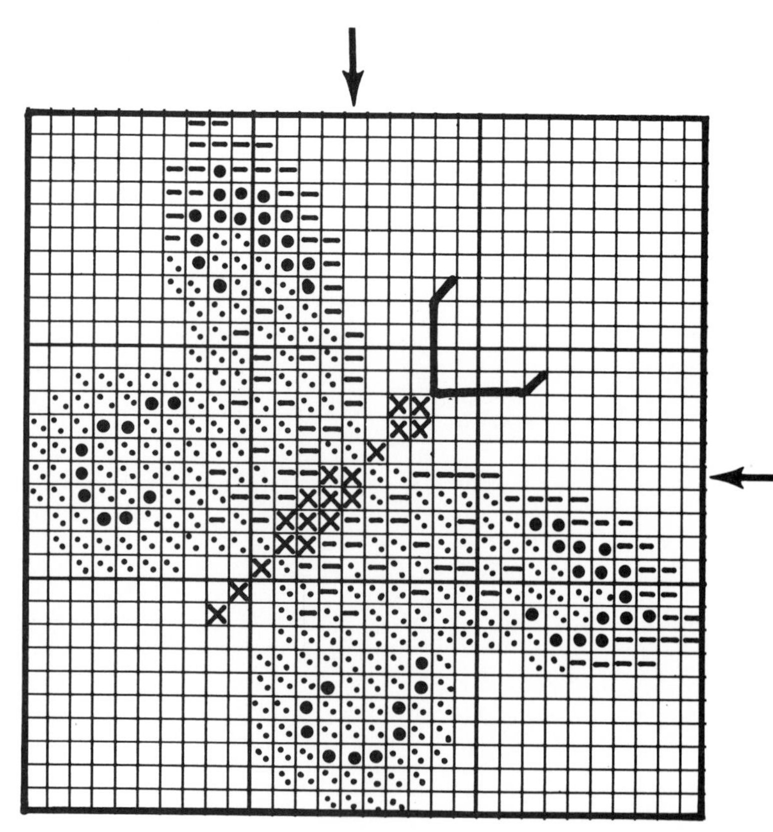

YELLOW BUTTERFLY
- Yellow #307 (4)
- Light Orange #972 (2)
- Dark Orange #740 (2)
- Medium Brown #434 (2)

Garden Wreath Prayer

Traditional motto, wreathed in flowers, will brighten the kitchen or breakfast nook.

"Give Us This Day"

SIZE:

Design area, about 9″ × 12″.

EQUIPMENT:

Masking tape. Ruler. Scissors. Straight pin. Tapestry needle. Embroidery hoop. Steam iron.

MATERIALS:

White 11-count Aida fabric, piece 15″ × 18″. DMC six-strand embroidery floss, one skein each color listed in color key.

DIRECTIONS:

Read Cross-Stitch How-To's, page 177. Prepare Aida cloth for embroidery. Place piece right side up on flat surface with short edges at top and bottom. Measure 3″ down from center of top edge and mark with pin for first stitch.

Following color key and symbols on chart, work design in cross-stitch with three strands floss in needle: Beginning at arrow, stitch right half of border; work left half of border in reverse, omitting vertical center row indicated by arrow. Work right half of wreath, the bow, and wheat sheaves as shown; work left half in reverse, continuing wreath at bottom left with vertical row indicated by star. Work cross-stitches of lettering.

Work additional embroidery, following heavy lines and dots on chart: With two strands dark brown, complete lettering with backstitching and French knots; see stitch details, page 178. With three strands, finish wheat with straight stitches and backstitching, using dark brown for "binding" and orange for remaining lines.

Finishing: Press finished embroidery well, wrong side up, on a padded surface. Mount and frame as desired.

"GIVE US THIS DAY"

- Rose #602
- Pink #604
- Orange #740
- Yellow #743
- Mustard #783
- Dark Brown #801
- Medium Blue #798
- Light Blue #809
- Dark Green #699
- Medium Green #702
- Light Green #704

Kitchen Treats from the Garden

Cover up small gifts with cross-stitch! Strawberries and grapes adorn jam jars, simple posies hide odds n' ends.

Odds n' Ends Basket

SIZE:

Basket, 3½″ inside diameter × 2″ high.

EQUIPMENT:

Masking tape. Straight pin. Embroidery hoop. Tapestry and sewing needles. Compass. Scissors.

MATERIALS:

Small woven basket with 3½″ inside diameter. Ivory 18-count Ainring fabric, piece 7″ square. DMC pearl cotton size 8, scraps of each color listed in color key, or desired colors. Stiff cardboard. Cotton fabric for back of lid, 5″ square. White craft glue. Scrap of batting. Ecru pregathered lace edging 1″ wide, 12″. Ecru sewing thread.

DIRECTIONS:

Read Cross-Stitch How-To's, page 177; prepare Ainring fabric as directed. To find center of fabric, fold in half lengthwise and crosswise; mark center with a pin. Place fabric in embroidery hoop. Follow chart to stitch design, beginning at arrow and working each cross-stitch over one "square" of fabric. When all cross-stitches are completed, work flower stems in backstitch (see stitch detail, page 178), following heavy lines on chart.

Remove fabric from hoop. Use compass to draw a 4″-diameter and a 3½″-diameter circle on cardboard; cut out both circles. Cut out two circles of batting, each slightly smaller than one of the cardboard circles. Glue batting to cardboard. Center embroidered piece, right side out, on larger circle with batting in between. Fold and glue edges of fabric to back of cardboard, using masking tape to hold fabric until glue dries. Remove tape and trim away excess fabric. Cover smaller circle with fabric in the same manner, for lid back. Glue lid back to lid front, centered, with wrong sides facing in. When glue is dry, stitch lace around edge of lid back, so that lace is visible around embroidered front.

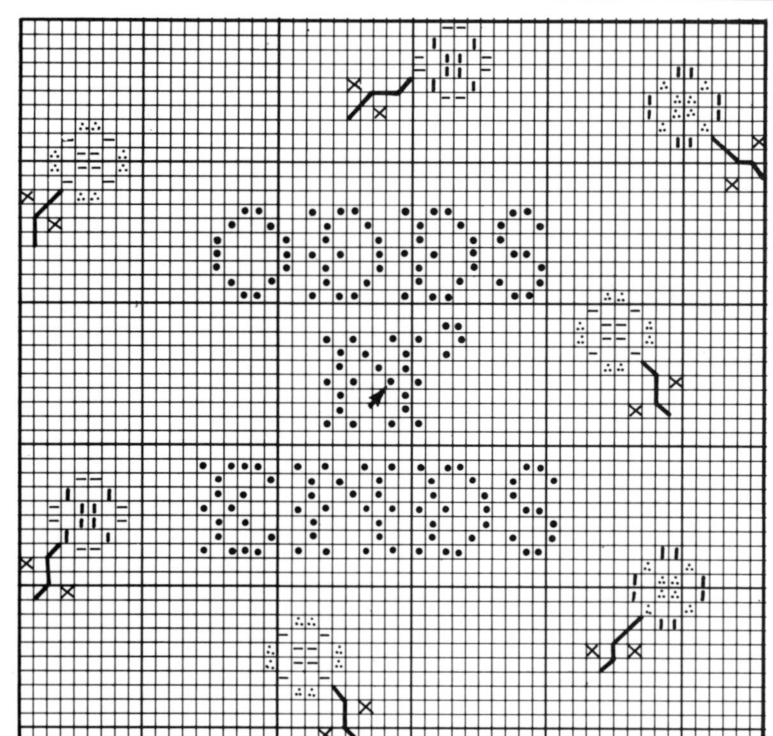

BASKET

- ● Blue #798
- ☒ Green #702
- ▮ Orange #946
- ⊟ Violet #553
- ⁘ Pink #602

Grape and Strawberry Jam Jar Covers

Shown on page 129

SIZE:

To fit a 2⅝″-diameter lid.

EQUIPMENT:

Embroidery hoop and needle. Straight pins. Compass. Scissors. Sewing machine. Iron.

MATERIALS:

For each: Jam jar with lid about 2⅝″ diameter. Blue/white gingham with about 14 checks-per-inch, piece 8″ square. DMC six-strand embroidery floss, one skein of each color listed in color key. White pregathered eyelet edging ¾″ wide, 19″. White sewing thread. Scrap of batting. Narrow rickrack in desired color, 21″. Rubber band.

DIRECTIONS:

For each: Read Cross-Stitch How-To's, page 177. Fold fabric in half lengthwise and crosswise to find center; mark center with a pin. Place fabric in embroidery hoop. Work design in cross-stitch, following chart and using three strands of floss in needle. Each square on chart represents one gingham square; work each cross-stitch in one gingham square, taking stitches in corners. Count away from center of fabric, indicated on charts by asterisk, to begin stitching.

When embroidery is completed, remove fabric from hoop. Use compass to draw a 6″-diameter circle on gingham, with embroidery in center. Pin bound edge of eyelet just inside circle so that ruffled edge faces embroidery. Stitch eyelet in place, then trim excess fabric to ½″ all around. Fold eyelet to outside and press excess fabric to back.

Cut a piece of batting same size as jar lid. Place batting on lid, then center embroidery on batting. Fold gingham down around sides of jar and secure with a rubber band, then tie rickrack in a bow, covering rubber band.

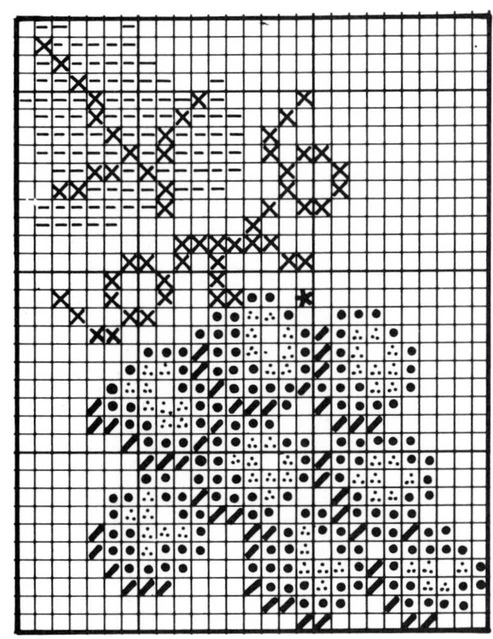

GRAPES

- ⊟ Light Green #704
- ⊠ Dark Green #701
- ◪ Plum #915
- ⊙ Violet #553
- ⁘ Lavender #554

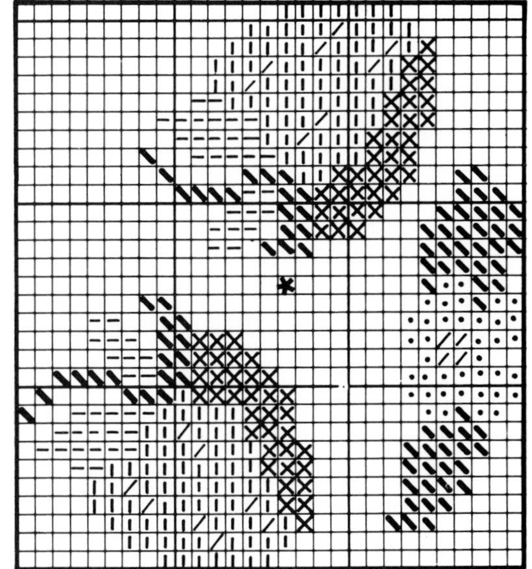

STRAWBERRIES

- ⊡ White
- ⊠ Red #666
- ⊟ Melon #892
- ⧅ Yellow #973
- ⎅ Light Green #704
- ◪ Dark Green #701

Country flowers for special moments . . .

Create cross-stitch heirlooms to celebrate the joys of life.

- The Elegant Wedding
- Wedding Celebration
- Wedding-Day Sampler
- Floral Wedding Treasures
- Floral Album Cover
- Morning Glory Birth Sampler
- Say it with Flowers
- Lavenders for My Sweetheart

opposite page: The Elegant Wedding

The Elegant Wedding

Exquisite ringbearer's pillow and rice bag are embroidered with delicate floral patterns and enhanced by a hardanger lattice. The bag becomes an elegant purse after the wedding.

Ring-Bearer's Pillow and Well-Wisher's Rice Bag

SIZES:

Pillow, about 11″ square; bag, about 7″ × 8″, plus handle.

EQUIPMENT:

Ruler. Straight pins. Scissors. Sewing needle. Contrasting basting thread. Tapestry needles, sizes 24 and 26. Very sharp embroidery scissors. Steam iron. Sewing machine. Magnifier (optional). **For Pillow:** Water-erasable marking pen. **For Bag:** Pushpin or tape.

MATERIALS:

White 22-count hardanger fabric, 43″ wide: ½ yard for pillow, ¼ yard for bag (½ yard will make both.) Matching sewing thread. Susan Bates Anchor® white pearl cotton: two 5-gram skeins size 5 and one 10-gram ball size 8 for pillow; one 5-gram skein size 5 and one 10-gram ball size 8 for bag (three skeins size 5 and one ball size 8 will make both). Light blue broadcloth 44″ wide: ⅜ yard for pillow, ¼ yard for bag. Matching sewing thread. Light blue satin ribbon 1⁄16″ wide: 1 yard for pillow, 1½ yards for bag. **For pillow:** Susan Bates Anchor® six-strand embroidery floss, one skein each color listed in color key, plus one skein each deep juniper #216, dark rose wine #894, and medium sea blue #977. White piping, 1½ yards. Fiberfill. **For bag:** Susan Bates Anchor® six-strand embroidery floss, one skein each light juniper #213, medium juniper #214, dark juniper #215, sandstone #885, light rose wine #892, medium rose wine #893, dark rose wine #894, and pale sea blue #975.

GENERAL DIRECTIONS:

Working Notes: Hardanger fabric is woven of 22 double threads-to-the-inch. Throughout these directions, illustrations, and charts, this double thread is referred to and shown as one thread. Read hardanger directions and study details on page 180. When embroidering, check frequently to be sure that Kloster blocks are directly across from one another and are worked over the same horizontal and/or vertical threads. The wrong side of your work should look very much like the right side, with no diagonal stitches. Accuracy in placing your stitches is essential for this type of embroidery.

Preparing Fabric: Pull one horizontal and one vertical fabric thread near edges to establish grainlines. With ruler, measure and mark piece as directed, measuring from pulled threads. Pull additional threads at markings, then cut along pulled threads on all four edges. By hand, overcast cut edges of piece to prevent raveling. With contrasting thread, hand-baste guidelines as individually directed.

(continued)

Kloster Blocks: Place prepared fabric on work surface. From intersection of guidelines, measure and mark starting point as individually directed below. Following project chart and hardanger directions on page 180, work blocks in a stair-step fashion around entire diamond motif back to starting point.

When first row of beginning diamond motif has been completed, count out and work second row, then remaining Kloster blocks on chart.

Cross-Stitch Motifs: Read Cross-Stitch How-To's, page 177. Work flower designs within hardanger borders in cross-stitch, following symbols on charts. Work each cross-stitch over one square of fabric threads, using one strand of floss in #26 needle. When cross-stitching is completed, work additional embroidery with one strand of floss as individually directed, following black outlines and dots on charts. For additional stitch details, see page 178.

Cutting Threads: Check alignment of blocks very carefully to be certain there are no mistakes. Following black lines on chart and using very sharp embroidery scissors, cut threads: Always keeping the Kloster block to the right of the scissors (unless you are left-handed), insert the tip of the blade into the bottom hole and bring it out four threads away at the corner hole. Check to be sure that you have picked up four threads, then snip as close to the block as possible without cutting the pearl cotton. Cut at all black lines on chart, then draw out the cut threads to create open squares plus groups of horizontal and vertical fabric threads.

Woven Bars and Dove's Eyes: Following charts and hardanger directions on page 180, work woven bars; then work a dove's eye in each square marked by a diamond on chart.

Finishing: Remove basted guidelines. Trim any thread ends on wrong side. Hand-wash piece, if necessary. Steam-press on a well-padded surface, right side up.

PILLOW

Read General Directions. Cut an 18″ square of hardanger fabric for pillow front. Baste guidelines along center threads in both directions, crossing at center of piece. Baste diagonal guidelines, dividing fabric into eight equal wedges.

For first stitch, place fabric on work surface with a straight edge parallel to table edge. Measure 3⅜″ down from center point along the diagonal guideline headed to the lower right corner of fabric; count two threads diagonally to the lower left and mark point with a pin for first stitch. Repeat the quarter-chart four times to complete the pillow top.

To complete the floral motifs, backstitch to outline flowers and buds with the darkest shade of matching color floss. Outline and vein large leaves with dark juniper; outline small leaves and sepals and work stems in deep juniper. Work light rose wine French knots where indicated by black dots on chart.

Assembly: With water-erasable pen and ruler, measure and mark cutting lines 1″ beyond the outer edges of embroidery. Cut along marked lines. Cut one same-sized square of hardanger fabric and two of broadcloth, placing squares on straight grain of fabrics.

(continued)

Place one square broadcloth, right side up, on a flat surface. Place embroidered pillow front, right side up, on broadcloth, matching edges; baste together ½″ from edges. Pin piping to edges of pillow front, placing right sides together and stitching line of piping at basting; stitch together with ½″ seam.

Baste remaining broadcloth square to wrong side of hardanger pillow back in same manner, omitting piping. Pin pillow front to back, right sides together; stitch with ½″ seam, leaving an opening for turning. Turn to right side. Cut ribbon in half; tack center of both pieces securely to center of pillow front. Holding both pieces together, tie ends into a bow. Stuff pillow with fiberfill; slip-stitch opening closed.

RING-BEARER'S PILLOW

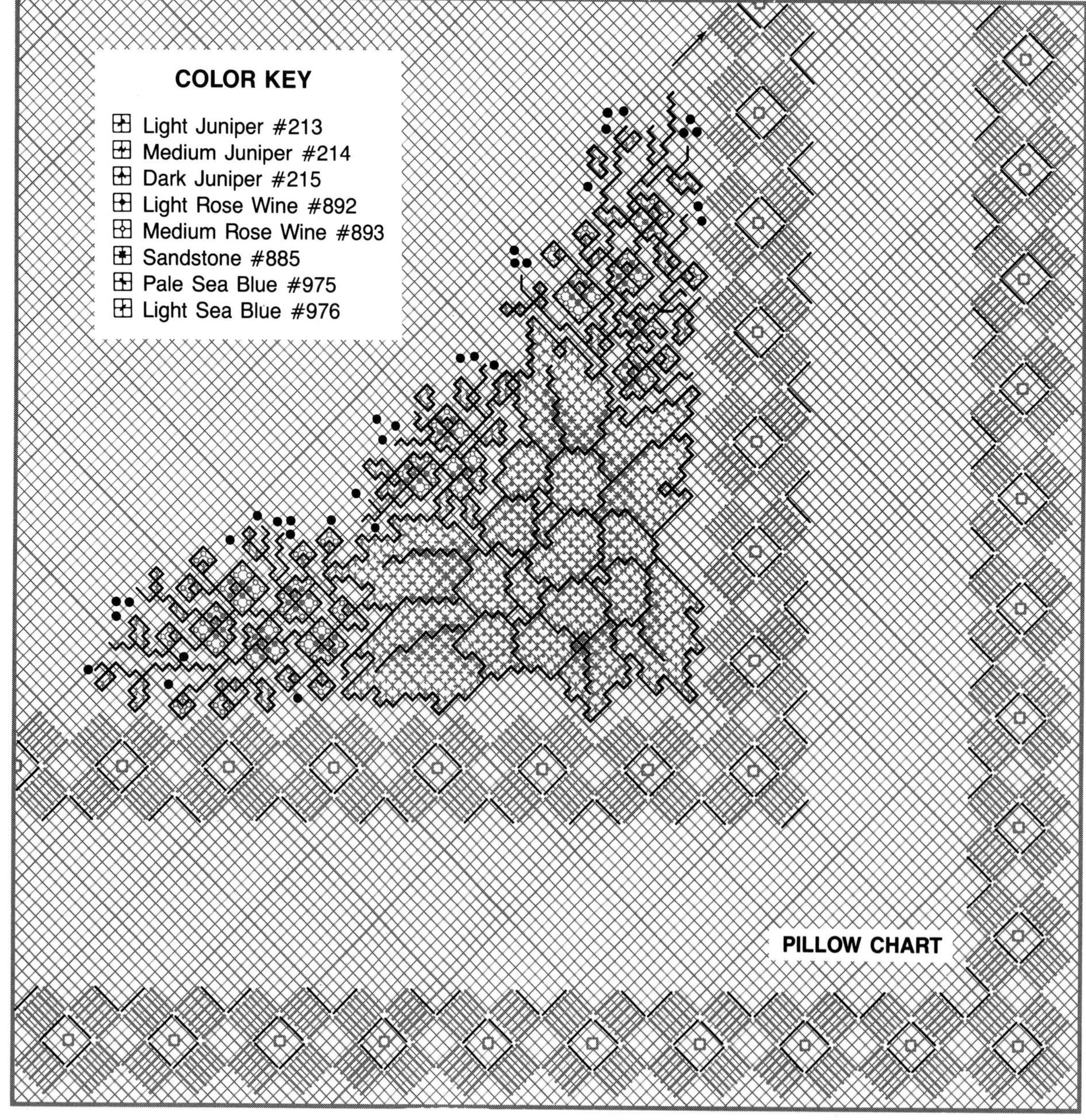

BAG

Read General Directions. Cut two 7½″ × 9″ pieces hardanger fabric; set one aside for bag back. Baste guideline along lengthwise center of bag front. Baste an intersecting horizontal guideline 4⅜″ from top edge of piece.

For first stitch, place piece on work surface with longer edges at sides and horizontal guideline 4⅜″ from top edge. From intersection of guidelines, measure 2¼″ down, then count two threads to the right and mark with pin for first stitch. Work entire chart from A to C, then reverse chart and work from B to A to complete block design.

Work floral motifs in each corner of diamond. Backstitch to outline flowers and buds in dark rose wine. Outline leaves and sepals with medium juniper; work stems in dark juniper. Work blue French knots where indicated by black dots on chart.

Assembly: Cut two 7½″ × 9″ pieces broadcloth for bag lining. Stitch bag front to back at side and bottom edges with ¼″ seam. To box corners, fold bag, matching side seam to bottom seam, and stitch across ½″ from corner; see diagram. Press top edges ¼″ to wrong side; turn bag right side out. Prepare lining in same manner as bag; do not turn. Slip lining into bag and slip-stitch folded edges together.

For cord, cut three three-yard pieces size 5 pearl cotton. Hold strands together with ends even; tie a tight overhand knot close to one end. Use pushpin or tape to secure knot on a fixed object. Twist strands together firmly in a clockwise direction until they begin to kink if tension is relaxed. Bring free end to knotted one, folding strands in half, and allow the two halves to twist together in a counterclockwise direction. Knot ends together. Beginning at a lower corner of bag with knotted end, slip-stitch cord over entire bag seamline, allowing extra cord to hang freely at top for handle.

Cut ribbon into four equal lengths. Tack the center of two pieces to each top corner of bag front about ¼″ in from edge. Tie ends of each pair of ribbons into a bow.

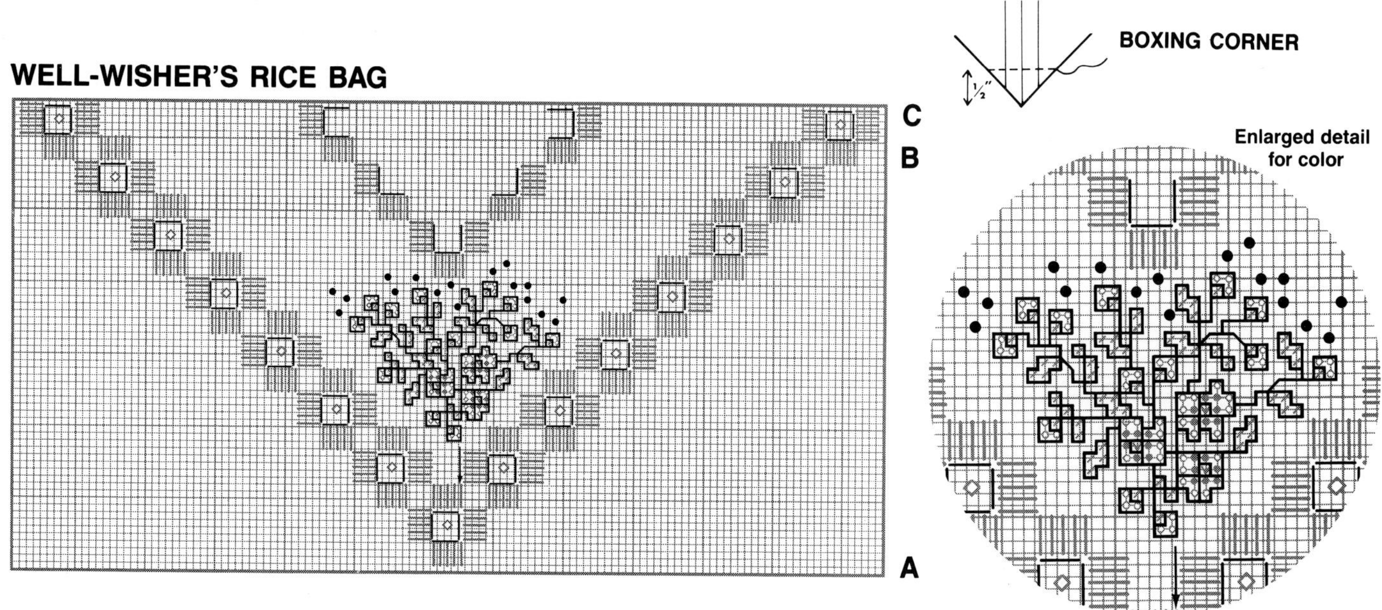

Wedding Celebration

Wedding celebration pictures, edged with hearts and flowers, make a thoughtful gift for a special couple.

Wedding Pictures

SIZE:
Each design area, $4\frac{1}{2}'' \times 6\frac{1}{2}''$.

EQUIPMENT:
Masking tape. Straight pin. Embroidery scissors and hoop. Tapestry needle. Iron.

MATERIALS:
White 14-count Aida fabric, piece $12'' \times 14''$ for each. DMC six-strand embroidery floss, one skein of each color listed in color key except white. DMC pearl cotton size 5, one skein white.

(continued)

DIRECTIONS:

Read Cross-Stitch How-To's, page 177; prepare fabric as directed. For each picture, measure 3¾″ down from top 12″ edge and 3¾″ in from left 14″ edge; mark thread with pin. Place fabric in hoop. Work each cross-stitch over one "square" of fabric, following charts and color key and using two strands of floss or one strand of white pearl cotton in needle; begin at pin with light blue stitch at upper left corner of border. Work white areas in half cross-stitch. After all cross-stitches are worked, complete other embroidery, using two strands

BRIDE AND BRIDESMAID

WEDDING PICTURES

- Flesh #754
- Yellow #727
- Tan #738
- Light Blue #827
- Medium Blue #799
- Light Pink #605
- Medium Pink #603
- Magenta #553
- Lilac #211
- Purple #209
- Green #703
- Light Brown #840
- Medium Brown #975
- Dark Brown #801
- Rust #919
- Gold #742
- White
- Black #310

of floss in needle, as follows: embroider all outlines, indicated by heavy lines on charts, with black backstitches; backstitch bride's necklace with gold floss; backstitch three sets of eyes with medium brown floss; ringbearer's eyes are medium blue cross-stitches. On ringbearer, work three black straight stitches for each side of bow tie, then work boot buttons with black French knots. See stitch details, page 178.

After all embroidery is completed, steam-press lightly on a padded surface; frame as desired.

GROOM AND RINGBEARER

- Flesh #754
- Yellow #727
- Tan #738
- Light Blue #827
- Medium Blue #799
- Light Pink #605
- Medium Pink #603
- Magenta #553
- Lilac #211
- Purple #209
- Green #703
- Light Brown #840
- Medium Brown #975
- Dark Brown #801
- Rust #919
- Gold #742
- White
- Black #310

Wedding-Day Sampler

Heart-strewn sampler will commemorate a marriage in charming style. Backstitched poem expresses the sweet sentiment.

Wedding-Day Sampler

SIZE:
Design area, 13⅞″ × 14″.

EQUIPMENT:
Masking tape. Ruler. Straight pin. Embroidery hoop. Tapestry and sewing needles. Embroidery scissors. Pencil. Tracing paper. Dressmaker's tracing (carbon) paper. Dry ball-point pen.

MATERIALS:
Ivory 22-count hardanger fabric, piece 18″ square. DMC six-strand embroidery floss, one skein of each color listed in color key, unless otherwise indicated in parentheses; also, one skein navy #312. Red plastic heart-shaped rhinestones approximately ⅜″ across, 18. White craft glue.

SAMPLER

Read Cross-Stitch How-To's, page 177, and see stitch details, page 178. Tape fabric edges to prevent raveling.

Place hardanger on a flat surface. Measure 2″ down and 3″ in from top left corner and mark with pin for first stitch. Place fabric in hoop, centering area to be worked and keeping fabric smooth and taut, with the grain straight. Work embroidery, following chart and color key. Each symbol on chart represents a cross-stitch worked over a square of two horizontal and two vertical fabric threads. Each line on chart represents a backstitch or straight stitch; see next paragraph for colors.

Beginning with stitch marked by arrow in upper left corner of chart, work border, birds, hearts, and tree in cross-stitch. Work solid lines on chart as follows: Using two strands of tan floss in needle, work flower pistils in straight stitch. Using three strands of copen blue floss, outline birds' wings and tail feathers in backstitch. Using two strands of floss, backstitch large-heart border in medium raspberry, small heart borders in light raspberry, and alphabet in azure. On a sheet of graph paper, plot initials and names desired, using letters in poem as a guide. Using two strands of navy floss, work poem, initials, and names in backstitch, working initials in large heart and centering names in area to right of tree (see color photograph); work ellipsis and dot the i's with French knots.

Block and mount sampler following Embroidery Basics, page 175. Glue two plastic hearts to sampler in each corner, covering cross-stitch hearts. Glue remaining hearts to tree at random to resemble apples; see color photograph.

abcdefghijklmnopq
vwxyz1234
one bride-one groom
one wedding tune
one tear-one smile
in quiet style
two touch two kiss
a future wish
one husband-one wife
for love & life
together
1
1

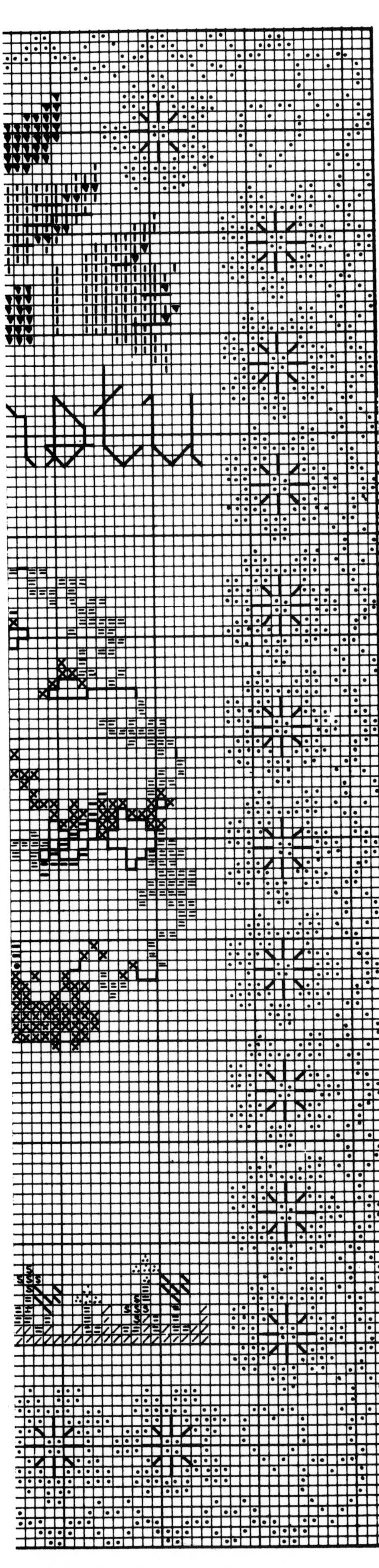

WEDDING SAMPLER

- Tan #739 (4)
- Azure Blue #3325
- Copen Blue #322
- Light Pistachio #368 (2)
- Medium Pistachio #320
- Dark Pistachio #319
- Light Raspberry #605
- Medium Raspberry #602
- Cranberry #498
- Light Amethyst #554
- Golden Brown #435
- Medium Brown #433

Floral Wedding Treasures

Floral cross-stitch motifs are always appropriate on wedding gifts. Choose one or all from our selection.

Wedding Day Picture Frame

SIZE:

Outer edges, 9¼″ × 9¾″; opening for picture, 3¾″ × 5½″.

EQUIPMENT:

Ruler. Pencil. Scissors. Tapestry and sewing needles, Embroidery hoop. Straight pin. Graph paper. Mat knife. Sewing machine.

MATERIALS:

White 22-count hardanger fabric, piece 12″ × 13″. DMC pearl cotton size 8, one skein of each color listed in color key. Masking tape. Batting. White craft glue. Scrap of white cotton fabric. Large scrap of printed cotton fabric. Sewing thread to match printed fabric. Thin, stiff cardboard. Light blue satin cord ⅛″ diameter, five feet. Ribbon to match printed fabric, 6″ piece.

DIRECTIONS:

Read Cross-Stitch How-To's, page 177; prepare hardanger fabric as directed. With short edges at top and bottom, measure 2¾″ down from top edge and 2¾″ in from left edge; mark thread with pin. Place fabric in hoop. Work design, following chart and color key; begin at pin with stitch marked by arrow on chart. Work each cross-stitch over two vertical and two horizontal fabric threads, using one strand of pearl cotton in needle. After design is completed, work monogram at bottom: Referring to name chart for wedding sampler on page 153, graph three initials, counting each square on graph paper as one horizontal and one vertical fabric thread; stitches for large center initial will be worked over two horizontal and two vertical fabric threads, while each smaller initial is worked over one horizontal and

(continued)

one vertical fabric thread. When initials are graphed, count squares across monogram and mark center square. On embroidery, measure distance between bottom ends of blue ribbon and mark center thread with pin. Embroider monogram in desired colors, lining up top of large initial with end stitches on ribbon and centering monogram along middle thread. After all embroidery is completed, remove fabric from hoop.

Using dark thread in sewing needle, baste along inside edge of embroidered frame (shown on chart by heavy line; remember to count each blank square as two threads). Mark a frame on cardboard; see "SIZE", page 147. Carefully cut out cardboard frame with mat knife; use as pattern to cut matching piece of batting. Glue batting to cardboard. Cut 6″ × 8″ piece white cotton fabric for facing. With right sides together and facing centered over embroidered piece, stitch close to basting line; remove basting. Cut away both layers of center rectangle to within 1/4″ of stitching line; snip into corners. Turn fabrics to right side; press. Pull facing through cardboard frame opening, with embroidered fabric on batting side and clipped seam allowance on cardboard side; seam should line up with inner edge of cardboard frame. Fold all edges to back of frame and glue in place, mitering corners. Glue satin cord to edges of frame as shown in photograph.

For back, mark rectangle on cardboard same size as front; cut out. Using cardboard back as pattern, cut printed cotton fabric 1″ larger than cardboard all around. Place fabric face down on surface; center cardboard on fabric back, then fold fabric edges over cardboard and tape or glue to back of cardboard. Cut three 1″-wide spacer strips from cardboard, two 9″ long for sides and one 5″ long for bottom. Glue strips to back of frame front; let dry. Spread glue on strips; press front and back pieces together, matching edges. Slip-stitch frame front to frame back along side and bottom edges.

For easel, cut a piece of printed cotton fabric 6″ × 7 1/4″; fold in half lengthwise, right side facing in, then stitch around long raw edge and one short edge, making 1/4″ seam. Turn to right side. Cut a 2 3/4″ × 6 3/4″ strip of cardboard. Draw a line across strip 1 1/2″ down from top edge and score along line with mat knife; insert cardboard in fabric. Fold in raw edges and slip-stitch opening closed. Center easel on back of frame so that scored cardboard folds out and bottom edge matches bottom edge of frame. Glue or slip-stitch top part of easel (down to scored fold) to back of frame. Glue ends of ribbon to frame back and easel back, 1/2″ from bottom of each piece.

WEDDING DAY PICTURE FRAME

- Dark Blue #806
- Light Blue #519
- Bright Blue #797
- Violet #553
- Pink #893
- Yellow #307
- Green #911

Silverware Rolls

Shown on pages 146-147

EQUIPMENT:

Ruler. Pencil. Regular and embroidery scissors. Tapestry needle. Masking tape. Embroidery hoop. Straight pins. Sewing machine. Steam iron.

MATERIALS:

For each: Pink 22-count hardanger fabric, piece 11″ × 16½″. DMC pearl cotton size 8: one skein each medium blue #798, light blue #800, pink #956, green #993 (enough for entire silverware set). Pink cotton flannelette, piece 18½″ × 16½″. Pink sewing thread. Light blue grosgrain ribbon ¼″ wide, 3″ piece.

DIRECTIONS:

Read Cross-Stitch How-To's, page 177; prepare fabric as directed. For each roll, measure 2½″ up from bottom short edge and 5½″ in from either long side; mark threads with pin. Place fabric in hoop. Work flower design, following chart and color key and beginning at pin with stitch marked by arrow on chart. Use one strand of pearl cotton in needle and work each cross-stitch over two horizontal and two vertical threads of fabric. When design is completed, cross-stitch lettering as follows: Count eleven threads up from top of light blue flower center to work first stitch marked by arrow on lettering chart, continuing to work over two threads; complete lettering following chart.

Finishing: After embroidery is completed, cut two flannelette pieces, 11″ × 16½″ and 7½″ × 16½″. Fold one long edge of 7½″ × 16½″ piece ¼″ to back twice and stitch a hem just above bottom of fold. With hem at top and starting 1¾″ from left edge, lightly mark eight straight lines 1¼″ apart across front of piece, using pencil and ruler. Pin marked piece to larger flannelette piece, both with right sides up and matching bottom and sides. Machine-stitch along each line to create eight narrow pockets and one wide pocket. Remove pins. Place embroidered piece on flannelette, right sides facing; pin, then stitch around all four edges, making ½″ seam and leaving an opening for turning at left edge. Turn to right side, slip-stitch opening closed, steam-press lightly. Tie 3″ ribbon into a small knot and tack to bottom front of roll as shown in color photograph.

RIBBAND PILLOWCASE AND TOWEL

- ☒ Green
- ⊡ Medium Orange
- ⊟ Light Orange
- ⊙ Blue

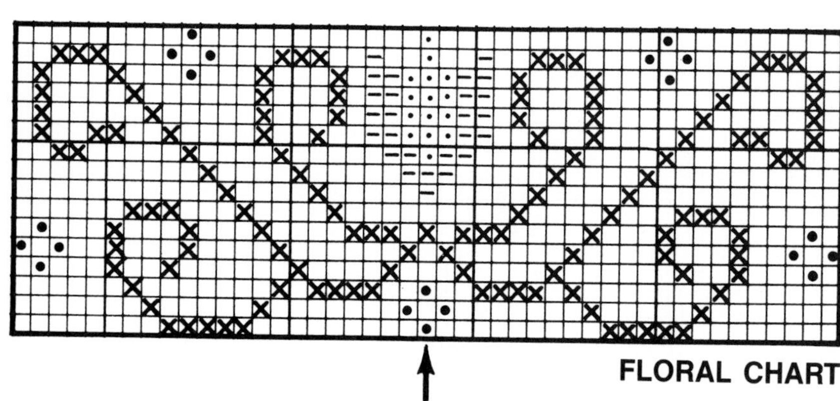

FLORAL CHART

SIVERWARE ROLLS

- ☒ Medium Blue
- ⊡ Light Blue
- ⊟ Pink
- ⊙ Green

Ribband™ Pillowcase and Towel

Shown on page 146

EQUIPMENT:

Ruler. Scissors. Tapestry needle. Straight pins. Sewing machine.

MATERIALS:

White pillowcase and towel. Mini-Weave Ribband™ from The Finish Line, ⅞" wide, white with blue scalloped edge, length to equal width of pillowcase and towel plus 2"; for mail order information, see Buyers' Guide, page 174. Pregathered white eyelet edging 1" wide, length to equal width of towel plus 1" and twice width of pillowcase plus 1". DMC six-strand embroidery floss: one skein each green #954, medium orange #352, light orange #353, blue #334. White sewing thread.

DIRECTIONS:

Read Cross-Stitch How-To's, page 177. Cut ribband into two pieces: the width of pillowcase plus 1" and the width of towel plus 1". To work design on ribband, fold each piece in half and mark center with a pin. Follow design chart for silverware rolls, but refer to ribband color key. Begin at center thread, two threads up from bottom border, with stitch marked by arrow on chart. Use one strand of floss in needle and work cross-stitches over one vertical and one horizontal fabric thread. When center motif is completed, count 23 threads to the right and left and work two more motifs.

Pin embroidered ribband across pillowcase or towel, 2¾" from edge, with raw edges overlapped on back side of pillowcase or folded ½" to back on each side for towel. Stitch in place along both edges of ribband. Pin eyelet edging all around open edge of pillowcase, overlapping ends; pin edging across bottom of towel, folding each raw edge ½" to back. Machine-stitch edgings in place.

LETTERING CHART

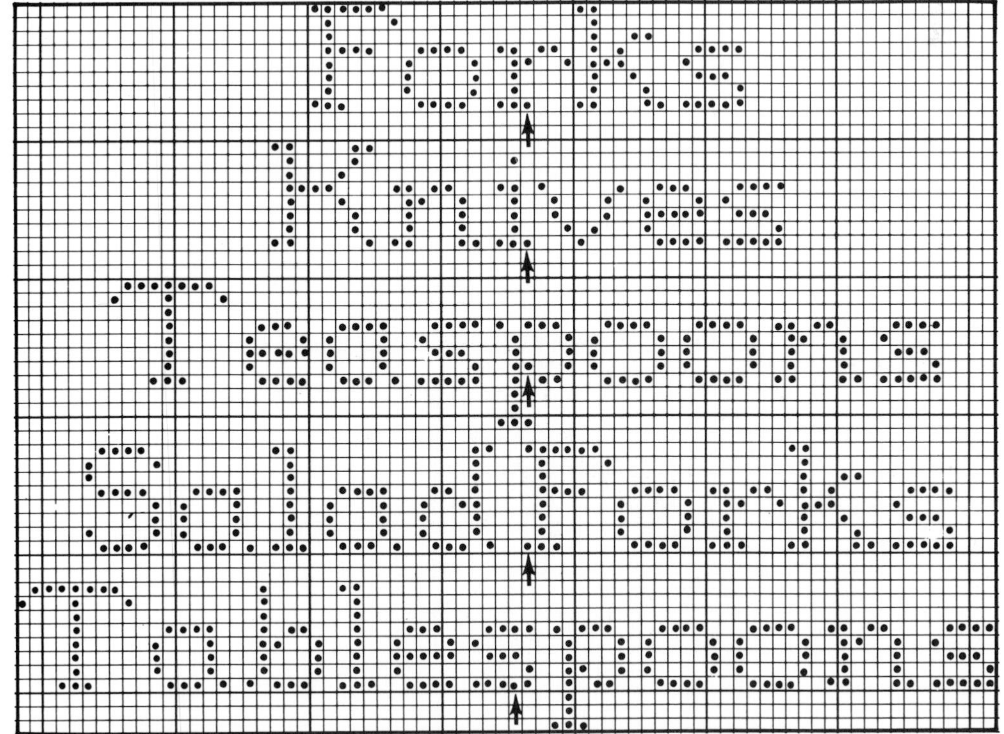

Wedding Sampler

Shown on page 147

SIZE:

Design area, 8¼″ × 8¾″.

EQUIPMENT:

Graph paper. Pencil. Masking tape. Straight pin. Tapestry needle. Embroidery scissors and hoop.

MATERIALS:

White 22-count hardanger fabric, piece 14″ square. DMC pearl cotton size 8, one skein of each color listed in color key, plus medium blue #797.

DIRECTIONS:

Before cross-stitching, plan your sampler on graph paper: First, draw a center vertical line on paper as an aid in centering each line. Chart lettering and date, using name and date charts given here (abbreviate month, if necessary); refer to color photograph for help in spacing letters and words.

Read Cross-Stitch How-To's, page 177; prepare fabric as directed. Fold fabric in half for vertical center, then mark line with long basting stitches. To begin embroidery, measure 4½″ down from top edge of fabric along basting thread; mark thread with pin (basting thread corresponds to center vertical line on your chart). Place fabric in hoop. Following your chart, work lettering and date with one strand of pearl cotton in needle, beginning at pin and alternating light and medium blues as shown. Each symbol on your chart represents one cross-stitch worked over two horizontal and two vertical fabric threads and blank squares represent two threads. For border, count up 27 stitches from top of lettering along center basting thread for placement of first stitch; mark thread with pin. With one strand of pearl cotton in needle, work border, following chart and color key and beginning at pin with stitch marked by arrow on chart. *Note:* Border can be widened if necessary to accommodate lettering by repositioning side flowers.

After all embroidery is completed, remove from hoop; frame as desired.

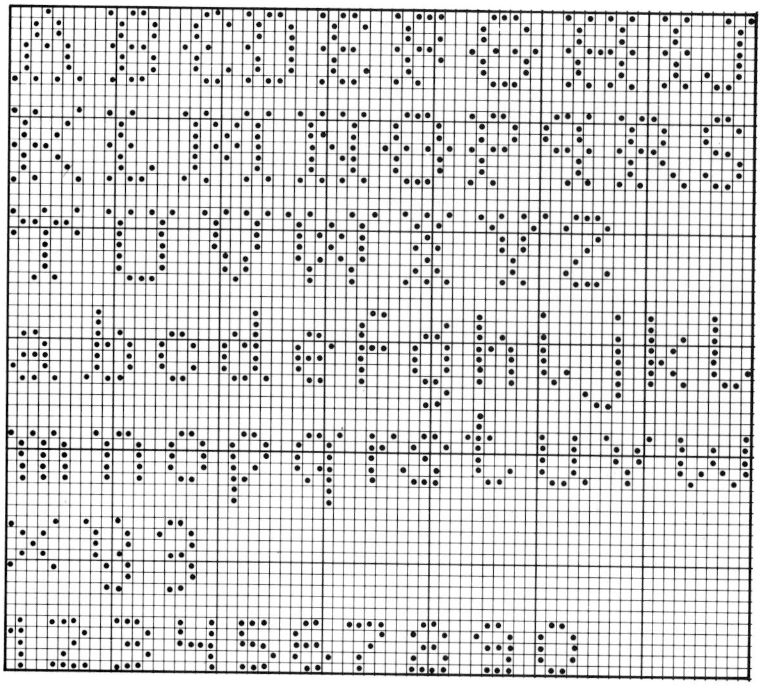

DATE CHART

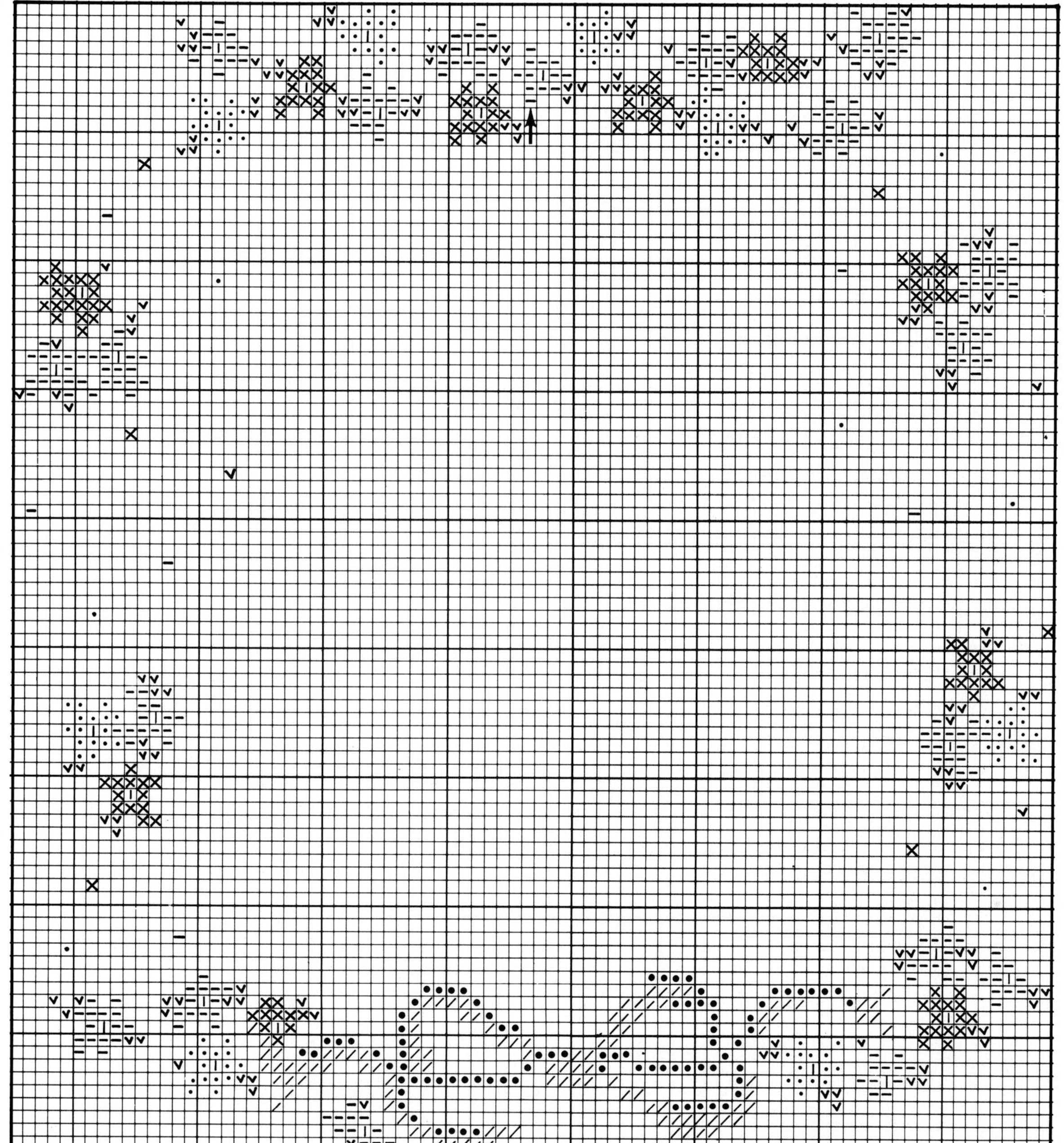

BORDER CHART

WEDDING SAMPLER

- Pink #604
- Light Blue #809
- Violet #553
- Green #913
- Yellow #307
- Brown #921
- Orange #741

NAME CHART

Floral Coasters

Shown on pages 146-147

SIZE:

3½″ diameter.

EQUIPMENT:

Ruler. Pencil. Scissors. Masking tape. Tapestry needle. Embroidery hoop. Iron.

MATERIALS:

For four: White 14-count Aida fabric, piece 10″ square. DMC pearl cotton size 8: one skein each medium blue #518, light blue #519, medium coral #893, light coral #948, yellow #743, green #912. One box white coasters for cross-stitch from Serendipity Designs; to order from Counted Thread, see Buyer's Guide, page 174. Iron-on interfacing, piece 8″ square.

DIRECTIONS:

Read Cross-Stitch How-To's, page 177. Fold fabric in half and cut along fold; fold each piece in half crosswise and cut along fold to make four 5″-square pieces. Tape fabric edges to prevent raveling. For each piece, count 28 threads down from top and 29 threads in from left side; mark thread with pin. Place fabric in embroidery hoop. To stitch design, use one strand of pearl cotton in needle and work each stitch over a "square" of one vertical and one horizontal fabric thread. To begin, place a green cross-stitch at thread marked by pin; this is green stitch at upper left of design. Following chart and color key, complete design.

When design is completed, cut interfacing into four 4″ squares; following manufacturer's instructions, iron one square to back of each embroidered piece, centered over design. Take apart one coaster; center clear top piece, right side up, over wrong side of embroidery and draw around edge of inner circle. Cut fabric along pencil line and place in coaster, right side up. Insert clear top piece of coaster over embroidery. Finish remaining coasters the same way.

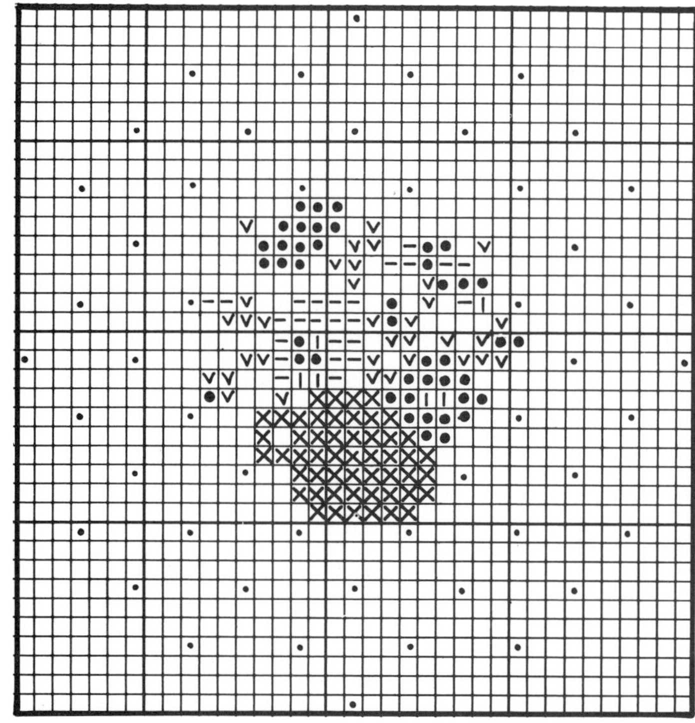

FLORAL COASTERS

- ☒ Medium Blue
- ⊡ Light Blue
- ● Medium Coral
- ⊟ Light Coral
- ⎅ Yellow
- ☑ Green

Sachets

Shown on pages 146-147

SIZES:

Bags, 5″ long; pillow 3″ × 3½″.

EQUIPMENT:

Ruler. Scissors. Masking tape. Straight pins. Tapestry needle. Embroidery hoop. Zigzag sewing machine. Iron.

MATERIALS:

For three bags: White 18-count Ainring fabric, piece 9″ × 13″. DMC pearl cotton size 8: one ball each dark pink #601, light pink #605, yellow #742, dark blue #796, light blue #518, green #905. Pink grosgrain ribbon ¼″ wide, 1¾ yards. **For pillow:** White 14-count Aida fabric, piece 4″ × 7″. DMC pearl cotton size 8: one ball blue #798, scraps of green #905 and pink #601. White pregathered lace edging ½″ wide, 14″. **For all:** White sewing thread. Purchased potpourri.

DIRECTIONS:

Read Cross-Stitch How-To's, page 177. Cut fabric as directed below; tape raw edges to prevent raveling. Find position of first stitch as directed below. Place fabric in hoop. Work design, following chart and color key. Use one strand of pearl cotton in needle, working cross-stitches over a "square" of one vertical and one horizontal fabric thread. Finish as directed.

Bags: For each bag, cut a piece of even-weave fabric 11½″ × 4″. Fold piece in half lengthwise and mark fold on one short edge (top) with a pin; unfold. To work Charts A and C, measure 2¼″ down from pin for first stitch indicated on charts by arrow; to work Chart B, measure 2¾″ down from pin.

When embroidery is completed, remove fabric from hoop. Press long edges of fabric ½″ to wrong side. Press each 4″ edge ¾″ to wrong side, then zigzag-stitch just inside raw edges to form two casings. Unfold sides, clipping into fabric at casings. Fold fabric in half crosswise, right side facing in; stitch sides up to casings, making ½″ seam. Turn bag right side out. Cut two 10½″ lengths of ribbon; insert one through each casing. Fill bag with potpourri, then tie a bow at each side of casing, gathering fabric to close bag.

Pillow: Cut even-weave fabric into two 3½″ × 4″ pieces; set one piece aside. Fold other piece in half lengthwise and crosswise to find center; mark thread with a pin. Choose an initial from the alphabet on the following pages. To find center of initial, count number of squares across chart and number of squares down (omitting tail for Q). Starting then at upper left corner, count half the depth down and half the width in to determine center stitch or space; mark on chart. Stitch initial, beginning at center of both chart and fabric and counting outward from center as you work. Work cross-stitches first, then work backstitch where indicated by solid lines on chart (see stitch detail, page 178).

When embroidery is completed, pin lace around edges of piece so that lace faces in with straight edge matching fabric edge. Stitch lace to fabric ⅛″ from edge; remove pins. Place second piece on top of first piece, right sides facing and matching edges. Sew around edges with ¼″ seams, leaving an opening for turning. Turn right side out, fill with potpourri, then slip-stitch opening closed.

- ● Dark Pink
- • Light Pink
- — Yellow
- ☒ Blue
- ◪ Green

CHART A

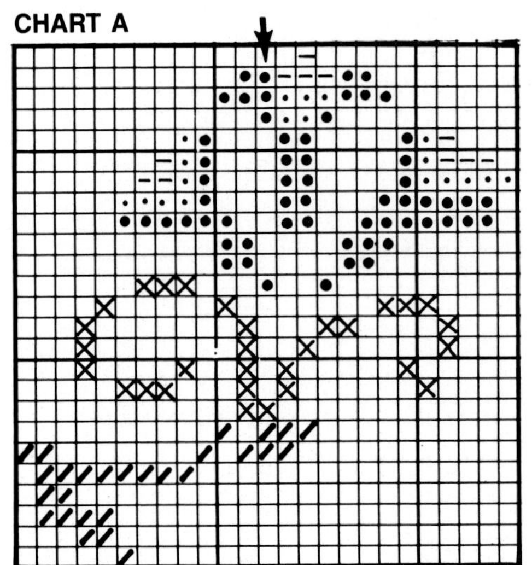

CHART B

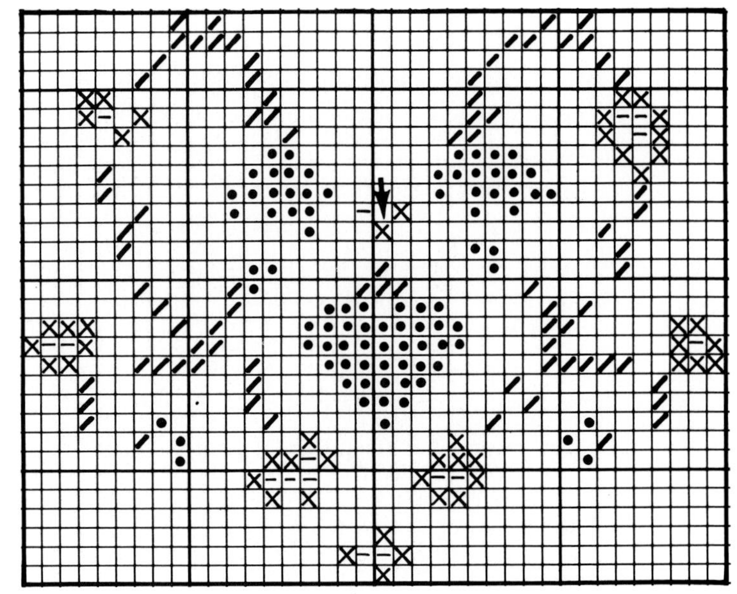

- ◪ Green
- ☒ Blue
- — Yellow
- ● Pink

CHART C

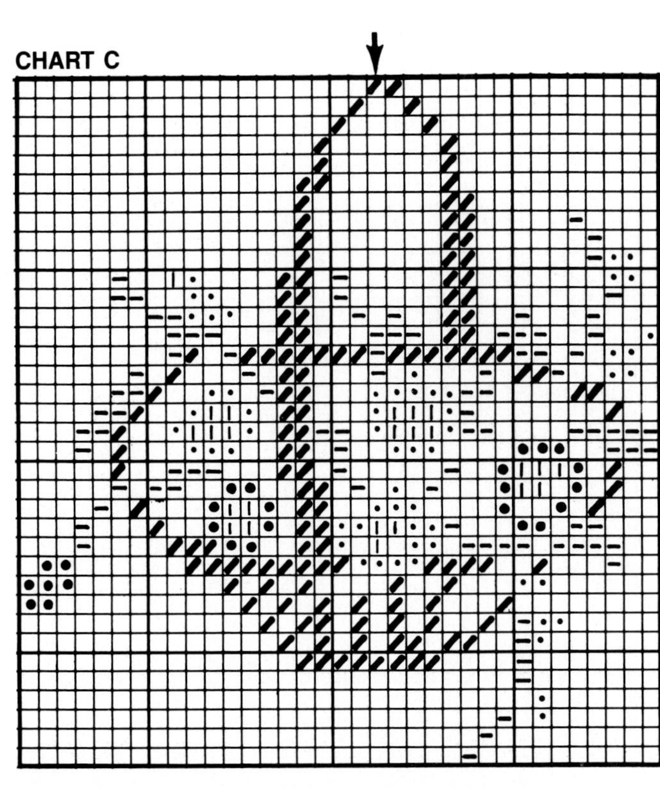

- ◪ Dark Blue
- ● Medium Blue
- • Pink
- | Yellow
- — Green

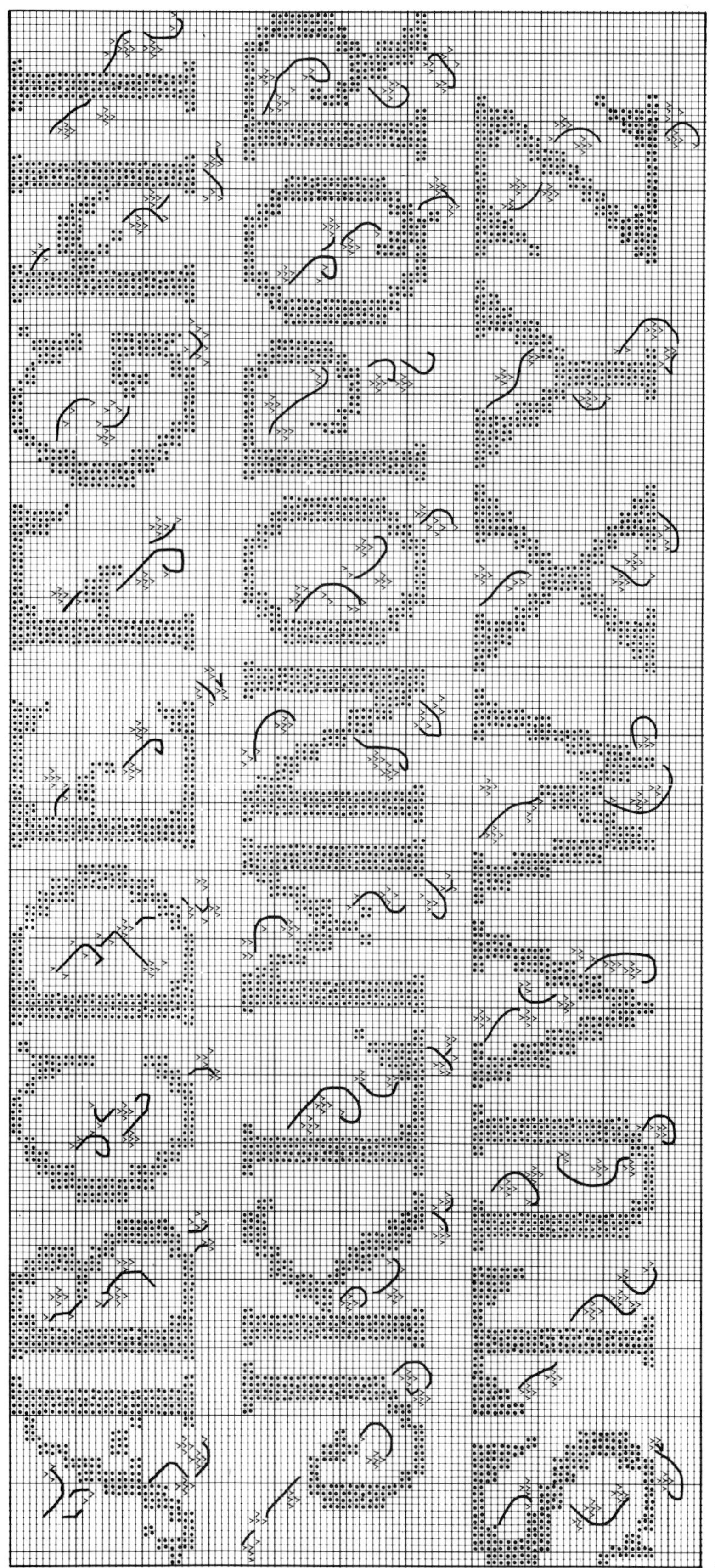

ALPHABET CHART FOR SACHETS

Floral Denim Album Cover

Graceful letters, flower sprigs, and a cross-stitched "dotted Swiss" pattern add old-fashioned appeal to this sturdy denim album cover.

Album Cover

SIZE:

Approximately 13″ × 14″.

EQUIPMENT:

Pencil. Ruler. Scissors. Sewing and embroidery needles. Embroidery hoop (optional). Penelope (cross-stitch) canvas, 10 mesh-to-the-inch, same size as album cover. Tweezers. For blocking: Brown paper. Soft wooden surface. T-square. Hammer. Thumbtacks.

MATERIALS:

Photo album, approximately 13″ × 14″, with removable covers. (*Note:* Covers attached with screws are recommended; if covers are tied, you will need grommets for the eyelets.) Blue denim fabric (see Directions for estimating amounts for your album). Six-strand embroidery floss (8.7-yard skeins): one skein each purple, red-orange, light green, dark green; three skeins pink. White craft glue.

DIRECTIONS:

Remove screws or ties from album cover. Measure front and back covers. Adding 2″ to width and doubling height, cut out denim for each cover. (*Note:* If album pages have a separate binding, cut fabric same measurement as width, ½″ longer at top and bottom.)

Using basting thread, outline size of album front on denim, having equal amounts of fabric at top and bottom, ½″ at center binding, 1½″ at outer edge. Center canvas within cover outline. Baste canvas to fabric.

See Four Methods of Cross-Stitching, page 177, for working cross-stitch over penelope canvas. Using four strands of floss in needle, follow chart and color key to work design. Add or subtract pink background crosses to enlarge or reduce design area to fit your album. When embroidery is finished, remove basting threads and use tweezers to remove penelope canvas.

Block embroidered piece following directions in Embroidery Basics, page 176.

To cover album, center back album cover on wrong side of corresponding denim. Bring excess at top and bottom to center of inside cover; glue firmly. Mitering corners and trimming at fold, bring fabric at outer edge to inside cover; glue in place. Turn excess fabric at center binding to inside cover; glue firmly in place. Repeat for front cover, being sure embroidery is positioned as desired. For binding on pages, glue fabric on original binding from edge to edge; turn ½″ at top and bottom to inside and glue firmly in place.

Using point of scissors, pierce fabric to accommodate screws. Use grommets to reinforce holes if necessary. Reassemble album.

FLORAL DENIM ALBUM

- ☒ Pink
- ⧅ Dark Green
- ◪ Purple
- ⊡ Light Green
- ▤ Red-Orange

Morning Glory Birth Sampler

Herald a child's birth with bright morning glories and a clean, simple alphabet.

Birth Sampler

SIZE:

Design area, approximately 11¼″ square.

EQUIPMENT:

Pencil. Ruler. Graph paper. Regular and embroidery scissors. Sewing and tapestry needles. Embroidery hoop. Straight pin. Steam iron.

MATERIALS:

Ecru 14-count Aida fabric, piece 16″ square. DMC six-strand embroidery floss, two skeins each color listed in color key, unless otherwise indicated in parentheses.

DIRECTIONS:

Before cross-stitching, plan your sampler on graph paper: First, draw a center vertical line on paper as an aid in centering each line. Chart lettering and date, using alphabet and numbers given here (abbreviate month, if necessary); refer to color photograph for help in spacing letters and words.

Read Cross-Stitch How-To's, page 177; prepare fabric as directed. Fold fabric in half for vertical center; mark line with long basting stitches.

To begin embroidery, measure 7¼″ down from top edge of fabric along basting thread; mark thread with pin (basting thread corresponds to center vertical line on your chart). Place fabric in hoop. Following your chart, work lettering and date with two strands medium blue floss in tapestry needle. Each symbol on your chart represents one cross-stitch worked over a "square" of one vertical and one horizontal fabric thread.

For border, count up 18 squares from top line of lettering along center basting thread for placement of first stitch; mark thread with pin. With two strands floss in needle, work border, following chart and color key, and beginning at stitch marked by arrow. Work backstitch (solid lines on chart) with dark yellow; see stitch details, page 178.

After all embroidery is completed, remove fabric from hoop and steam-press gently on a padded surface. Mount and frame as desired.

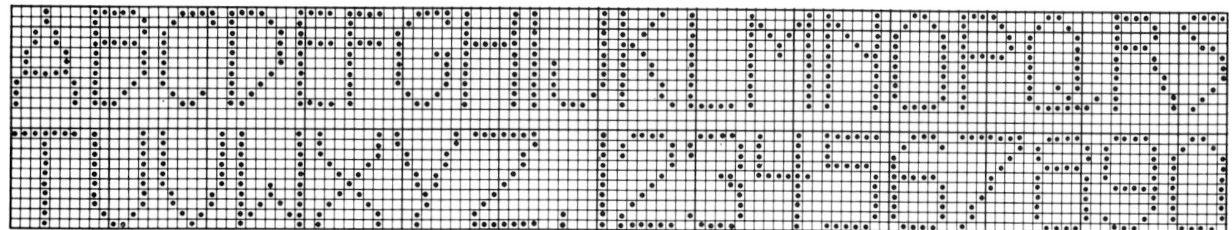

- Light Blue #800
- Medium Blue #799 (3)
- Dark Blue #798
- Light Green #368
- Medium Green #320
- Dark Green #319
- Medium Yellow #726 (1)
- Dark Yellow #725 (1)
- White (1)

BIRTH SAMPLER

Say it with Flowers

Say "I Love You" with hearts and flowers. The tender sentiments on these pillows are surrounded by colorful ribbon trim.

Mother, Grandmother and Sister Pillows

SIZES:

(without ruffles) "Sister" pillow, about 14" diameter; "Mother" pillow, about 12" × 15"; "Grandmother" pillow about 11" × 14".

EQUIPMENT:

Pencil. Ruler. Masking tape. Scissors. Tapestry needle. Embroidery hoop. Water-erasable pen. Tracing paper. Sewing needle. Sewing machine. Straight pins. Steam iron.

MATERIALS:

For each pillow: White 11-count Aida fabric, piece 19" square. DMC six-strand embroidery floss, one skein each color in color key, unless otherwise indicated in parentheses. Cotton broadcloth 44" wide, 1 yard (for backing and ruffle). White pregathered lace: 1¾" wide, 1½ yards; ¾" wide, including beading panel at one edge, 1 yard. Satin ribbon ⅛" wide, 1¼ yards (for threading through beading panel). Sewing threads to match broadcloth and lace. Fiberfill.

DIRECTIONS:

Read Cross-Stitch How-To's, page 177. Prepare Aida cloth for embroidery. Fold piece in quarters to locate center; mark center for placement of first stitch. Work designs in cross-stitch, using three strands floss in needle. Work lettering and center motifs first, then border. Work additional embroidery for each pillow as follows (see stitch details, page 178);

For "Sister" Pillow: Use three strands dark peacock blue to work vertical lines in backstitch. Use two strands black to add straight stitch accents on pansies, in medium amethyst area.

For "Mother" Pillow: Use three strands dark pink to work zigzag lines in straight stitch or backstitch. Use four strands to work vertical lines in gold backstitch. Use four strands to work French knot flowers, using medium peacock blue for petals and dark pink for centers; work knots in center of fabric squares as shown, rather than at intersections.

For "Grandmother" Pillow: Starting at upper left corner and continuing clockwise around border, number patches 1—14. Use three strands floss to work the following in straight stitch or backstitch: Turquoise zigzag lines in patch 2; apple green upright crosses in patch 4; apple green flower stems and leaves in patches 6, 9, and 13, and in center section; orange diagonal lines in patch 14. Use four strands orange to work French knots in patch 11. Use two strands brown to work running stitch between patches, following solid lines on chart and working between squares of fabric; do not stitch inner and outer edges of border.

Finishing: When all embroidery is complete, press piece gently face down on padded surface. On right side, use water-erasable pen to mark inner and outer border edges, following heavy lines on chart: Mark lines along rows of holes for "Grandmother" pillow; use compass to mark circles on "Sister" pillow; use tracing paper to make sure left and right halves of heart are symmetrical on "Mother" pillow. For each pillow, baste outer edge of border only, to mark wrong side.

To Add Beading Lace: Cut ¾" lace to fit around inner border, plus ½"; press ends under ¼". Starting and ending at center top, pin lace in place on pillow front with beading panel facing center; topstitch. Do not insert ribbon until directed.

(continued)

"MOTHER" PILLOW

- ⁘ Gold #742
- ▭ Orange #740
- ☒ Fuchsia #600
- ⧄ Dark Pink #603
- ● Medium Peacock Blue #996
- ▯ Apple Green #704
- ☑ Kelly Green #701 (2)

To Make Pillow: Trim away Aida fabric beyond basting to ½″. Cut pillow back from broadcloth. Cut 6″-wide broadcloth ruffle twice as long as perimeter of pillow front. Construct pillow with ruffle, enclosing wide lace in seam; for directions, refer to Sewing Hints, page 181.

Using tapestry needle, thread ribbon through beading panel, beginning and ending at center top. Tie bow as shown.

"GRANDMOTHER" PILLOW

- Yellow #743 (2)
- Orange #740 (2)
- Dark Pink #603 (2)
- Turquoise #597 (2)
- Aquamarine #518
- Light Amethyst #554 (2)
- Apple Green #704 (2)
- Brown #869

"SISTER" PILLOW

- C Gold #742
- V Medium Pink #604 (2)
- Magenta #718
- Light Amethyst #554
- = Medium Amethyst #552
- X Lavender #208
- – Medium Peacock Blue #996
- 6 Dark Peacock Blue #995
- I Apple Green #704
- ● Kelly Green #701
- Black #310

Lavenders for My Sweetheart

Surprise your sweetheart with a delightful, heart-framed picture or an unusual "Hug Me" heart.

Sweetheart Sampler

SIZE:
Framed, 11″ × 12½″, plus trim.

EQUIPMENT:
Pencil. Ruler. Paper for pattern. Embroidery and regular scissors. Mat knife. Embroidery hoop. Tapestry needle. Straight pins. Dressmaker's tracing (carbon) paper. Dry ball-point pen. Iron.

MATERIALS:
Off-white 18-count Ainring fabric, 10″ × 10½″. DMC six-strand embroidery floss, one skein each color in color key unless otherwise indicated in parentheses. Sturdy cardboard or mat board. Closely woven cotton fabric 44″ wide, ½ yard ecru-on-lavender dotted. Sewing thread to match fabric. Ecru pre-gathered lace trim ½″ wide, 2¼ yards. Ecru satin ribbon ⅜″ wide, ¼ yard. Batting. White craft glue.

DIRECTIONS:
Read Cross-Stitch How-To's, page 177. Prepare Ainring fabric as directed. For first stitch, place piece with short edges at top and bottom and measure 3¼″ up from center bottom; mark fabric thread with pin. Place piece in hoop. Work design following chart and color key and beginning with stitch indicated by arrow. Each symbol on chart represents one cross-stitch worked over one "square" of fabric; different symbols represent different colors. Solid lines represent backstitches, each to be worked the length of one square of fabric after cross-stitch embroidery is completed (see stitch detail, page 178). Separate floss and work with two strands in needle throughout. Work cross-stitches, using flesh for faces, neck, and hands and leaving background unworked. Backstitch mouths with rose. Outline hands, crowns, and crown jewels in backstitch with dark gray. Outline queen's hair with light gray. Work lettering with dark lavender. After all embroidery is completed, remove fabric from hoop. Press gently face down on a padded surface.

To Make Frame: Draw lines across heart pattern, connecting grid lines. Enlarge pattern by copying on paper ruled in 1″ squares. Complete half-pattern indicated by dash line.

On cardboard, mark 11″ × 12½″ rectangle. With long edges of rectangle at sides, transfer heart to center, using dressmaker's carbon and dry ball-point pen. Cut on marked lines, using mat knife. From fabric, cut one piece 15″ × 16½″ (frame front) and one piece 10″ × 11½″ (facing). Use cardboard frame as pattern to mark heart on wrong

(continued)

Lavender's Blue, dilly, dilly,
Lavender's Green;
When I'm a king, dilly, dilly,
You shall be queen!
I LOVE YOU THIS MUCH

side of facing, centering it. Cut piece of batting to match frame; glue to cardboard. Center facing on frame front, right sides together, and pin. Stitch along heart outline. Cut away heart to within ¼″ of stitching; slip into seam allowance at curves. Turn fabrics to right side; press. Pull facing through cardboard opening, with frame front on batting side and clipped seam allowance on cardboard side; seam should line up with inner edges of frame. Fold all edges to back of frame and glue in place, mitering corners. Cut lace to fit around outer and inner frame edges, adding ½″ to each measurement for overlap. Glue lace behind frame so that ruffles extend ⅜″ beyond frame edges. Place embroidered piece behind frame, centering design area within opening; glue in place.

For frame back, cut piece same size as front piece from cardboard; use as pattern to mark one piece on fabric; cut out at least 1″ outside marked lines for fold allowance. Center cardboard on wrong side of fabric; fold fabric margins over edges and glue in place. Glue frame front and back together.

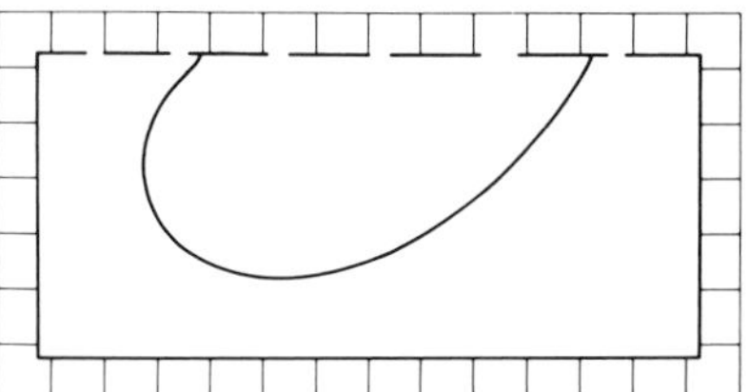

Lavender's Blue, dilly, dilly,
Lavender's Green;
When I'm a king, dilly, dilly,
You shall be queen!

LAVENDER'S BLUE

- ● Dark Lavender #553 (2)
- I Light Lavender #210
- ≡ Rose #3350
- — Pink #604
- □ Flesh #948
- + Honey #422
- X Dark Green #3345
- ∴ Light Green #3348
- ◣ Dark Gray #413
- ⟍ Light Gray #318
- ■ Black #310

"Hug-Me" Heart

Shown on page 170

SIZE:

8″ × 3¾″.

EQUIPMENT:

Ruler. pencil. Tracing paper. Dressmaker's tracing (carbon) paper. Dry ball-point pen. Straight pins. Small embroidery hoop. Scissors. Tapestry and sewing needles. Iron. Sewing machine.

MATERIALS:

White 14-count Aida fabric, piece 6″ × 6″. White-and-purple printed cotton fabric such as batiste or percale, piece 6″ × 4″. White sewing thread. DMC six-strand embroidery floss: one skein each purple #208, mauve #223, blue #793, gray #413, green #502. Fiberfill.

DIRECTIONS:

Read Cross-Stitch How-To's, page 177; prepare Aida fabric as directed. Measure 1⅛″ down and 1½″ in from top left corner; mark thread with pin. Work design in cross-stitch, following chart and color key; begin at pin with stitch marked by arrow on chart. Each symbol on chart represents a cross-stitch. Work each cross-stitch over one "square" of fabric, separating strands of embroidery floss and using three strands in tapestry needle. When cross-stitching is completed, work heavy lines in backstitch (see stitch detail, page 178): Work "I Love You This Much" with gray; work flower stems at top center with green. After all embroidery is completed, remove fabric from hoop. Steam-press gently on padded surface.

From purple printed fabric, cut a strip 5¾″ × 1″. Fold strip lengthwise, right side on the inside, matching long edges. Machine-stitch ¼″ from long edges. Trim ⅛″ beyond stitching. Turn to right side and press. Set aside for hanging loop.

Trace actual-size arm pattern. Use dressmaker's tracing (carbon) paper and dry ball-point pen to transfer four arm outlines to wrong side of white fabric: Position arms ½″ from edges and ½″ apart; reverse second and fourth pieces. Hand-baste tiny stitches around mitt part of each hand. Turn fabric to right side and, using basting as a guide, transfer dotted lines to fabric. Remove basting. Cut out arms ¼″ beyond marked edges. Place one arm piece and its reversal right sides together and stitch ¼″ from edges; leave edge opposite fingers open. Turn to right side. Stuff lightly with fiberfill. Baste raw edges together. Machine-stitch along dotted lines through all thicknesses for fingers, backstitching at beginning and end of each line to secure. Make second arm in same manner; set both arms aside.

Turn cross-stitched fabric to wrong side. Following outline of chart, mark heart outline, rounding out curves. (*Note:* Leave edge at top center flat for hanging loop.) Cut ¼″ beyond marked line for heart front. Use this piece as a pattern to cut heart back from remaining purple fabric. Holding heart front right side up, position raw edges of one arm against raw edge of heart so that arm aligns with "I Love You This Much" and thumb points up. Baste ¼″ from edges. Repeat for second arm. Place raw ends of purple strip against heart at top center and baste ¼″ from edge. Place heart back and heart front together, right sides facing, with arms and loop on the inside; pin. Machine-stitch through both thicknesses, ¼″ from edges, catching arms and loop in seam and leaving a 1″ opening for turning along lower edge. Turn, stuff heart with fiberfill, and slip-stitch opening closed.

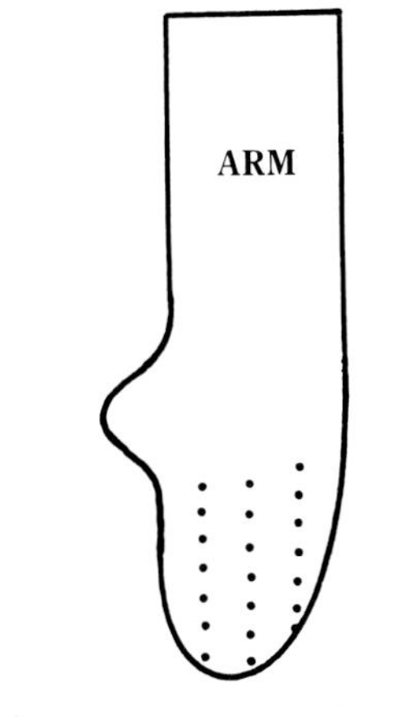

ACTUAL-SIZE PATTERN

"HUG-ME" HEART

- ☒ Purple #208
- ⚀ Mauve #223
- ⊟ Blue #793
- ⊞ Gray #413
- ⊙ Green #502

Country cross-stitch basics...

Master the ABC's of cross-stitch, and enjoy many years of creative stitchery.

- Buyers' Guide
- Embroidery Basics
- Cross-Stitch How-To's
- Embroidery Stitch Details

Buyers' Guide

CHARLES CRAFT, INC.
P.O. Box 1049
Laurinburg, NC 28352

COUNTED THREAD
200 Turner Road
Richmond, VA 23225

CRAFT GALLERY, LTD.
P.O. Box 541
New City, NY 10956

THE DAISY CHAIN
P.O. Box 1258
Parkersburg, WV 26102

THE FINISH LINE
P.O. Box 2712
Spartanburg, SC 29304

HANSI'S HAUS
35 Fairfield Place
West Caldwell, NJ 07006

SUDBERRY HOUSE
Four Mile and Colton Roads
Box 895
Old Lyme, CT 06371

WHEATLAND CRAFTS, INC.
Rte. 5, Scuffletown Road
Simpsonville, SC 29681

For mail order information, send your request with a self-addressed envelope to the companies listed above.

Embroidery Basics

THREADING THE NEEDLE: To thread yarn or floss through the needle eye, double it over the end of the needle and slip it off, holding it tightly as close as possible to the fold. Push the eye of the needle down over the folded end and pull the yarn through.

TO BEGIN A STITCH: Start your embroidery with two or three tiny running stitches toward the starting point, then take a tiny backstitch and begin. Do not make knots when beginning or ending stitches.

TO END A COLOR: Fasten off the thread when ending each motif, rather than carrying it to another motif. Pass the end of the thread through the last few stitches on the wrong side, or take a few tiny backstitches.

TO REMOVE EMBROIDERY: When a mistake has been made, run a needle, eye first, under the stitches. Pull the embroidery away from the fabric; cut carefully with scissors pressed hard against the needle. Pick out the cut portion of the embroidery. Catch loose ends of the remaining stitches on back by pulling the ends under the stitches with a crochet hook.

TO FINISH: When your embroidered piece is complete, finish off the back neatly by running ends into the back of the work and clipping off any excess strands. If wool embroidery is not really soiled but needs just a little freshening, simply brushing over the surface with a clean cloth dipped in carbon tetrachloride or another good cleaning fluid may be satisfactory. This will brighten and return colors to their original look. If fabric is soiled, wash gently. Embroideries made of colorfast threads and washable fabrics can be laundered without fear of harming them. Wash with mild soap or detergent and warm water, swishing it through the water gently—do not rub. Rinse in clear water without wringing or squeezing. When completely rinsed, lift from the water and lay on a clean towel; lay another towel on top and roll up loosely. When the embroidery is sufficiently dry, press as described below.

Finishing Techniques

Better results will be obtained by blocking rather than pressing an embroidered piece for a picture or hanging. However, articles that are hemmed, such as tablecloths or runners, should be pressed; blocking would damage the edge of the fabric. To press your embroidered piece, use a well-padded surface and steam iron, or regular iron and damp cloth. Embroideries that have been worked in a frame will need very little pressing. If the embroidery was done in the hand it will no doubt be quite wrinkled and may need dampening. Sprinkle it to dampen and roll loosely in a clean towel. Embroidery should always be pressed lightly so that the stitching will not be flattened into the fabric. Place the embroidered piece face down on the padded surface and press from the center outward. For embroidery that is raised from the surface of the background, use extra thick, soft padding, such as a thick blanket.

After blocking or pressing, an embroidered picture should be mounted right away to prevent creasing.

TO BLOCK:

Using needle and colorfast thread, follow the thread of the linen and take ¼″ stitches to mark guidelines around the entire picture, designating the exact area where the picture will fit into the rabbet of the frame. The border of plain linen extending beyond the embroidery in a framed picture is approximately 1¼″ at sides and top and 1½″ at bottom. In order to have sufficient linen around the embroidered design for blocking and mounting, 3″ or 4″ of linen should be left around the embroidered section. Now, matching corners, obtain the exact centers of the four sides and mark these centers with a few stitches.

If the picture is soiled, it should be washed, but it should be blocked immediately after washing. In preparation, cover a drawing board or soft wood breadboard with a piece of brown paper held in place with thumbtacks, and draw the exact original size of the linen on the brown paper. Be sure linen is not pulled beyond its original size when the measurements are taken. (Embroidery sometimes pulls linen slightly out of shape.) Check drawn rectangle to make sure corners are square.

Wash embroidery; let drip a minute. Place embroidery right side up on the brown paper inside the guidelines and tack down the four corners. Tack centers of four sides. Continue to stretch the linen to its original size by tacking all around the sides, dividing and subdividing the spaces between the tacks already placed. This procedure is followed until there is a solid border of thumbtacks around the entire edge. In cross-stitch pictures, if stitches were not worked exactly even on the thread of the linen, it may be necessary to remove some of the tacks and pull part of embroidery into a straight line. Use a ruler as a guide for straightening the lines of stitches. Hammer in the tacks or they will pop out as the linen dries. Allow embroidery to dry thoroughly.

TO MOUNT:

Cut a piece of heavy white cardboard about ⅛″ smaller all around than the rabbet size of the frame to be used. Stretch the embroidery over the cardboard, using the same general procedure as for blocking the piece. Following the thread guidelines, use pins to attach the four corners of the embroidery to the mounting board. Pins are placed at the centers of sides, and embroidery is then gradually stretched into position until there is a border of pins completely around picture, about ¼″ apart. When satisfied that the design is even, drive pins into the cardboard edge with a hammer. If a pin does not go in straight, it should be removed and reinserted. The edges of the linen may be pasted or taped down on the wrong side of the cardboard or the edges may be caught with long zig-zag stitches. Embroidered pictures can be framed with glass over them if desired.

Cross-Stitch How-To's

To prevent fabric from raveling, bind all raw edges with masking tape, whipstitch edges by hand, or machine-stitch ⅛" in from all edges. Work embroidery in a frame or hoop to keep fabric taut; move hoop as needed. Cut floss or yarn into 18" lengths. To begin a strand, leave an end on back and work over it to secure; to end, run needle under four or five stitches on back of work.

Each symbol on chart represents one cross-stitch. Different symbols represent different colors. When working cross-stitches, work all underneath stitches in one direction and all top stitches in the opposite direction, making sure all strands lie smooth and flat; allow needle to hang freely from work occasionally to untwist floss. Make crosses touch by inserting needle in same hole used for adjacent stitch (see stitch detail).

Several different ways to do cross-stitch are described below. All yield equally good results if care is taken to make sure that the strands of threads or yarn lie smooth and flat.

Four Methods of Cross-Stitching

Monk's or Aida Cloth: The design can follow the mesh of a coarse, flat-weave fabric, such as monk's cloth. Here the design may be worked from a chart simply by counting each square of fabric for one stitch.

Gingham: A checked material, such as gingham, can be used as a guide for cross-stitch. Crosses are made over checks, following a chart.

Even-Weave Fabric: The threads of an even-weave fabric, such as sampler linen, may be counted and each cross-stitch made the same size.

Penelope Canvas: Penelope (or cross-stitch) canvas is basted to the fabric on which the design is to be embroidered. First, center canvas over fabric, making sure that horizontal and vertical threads of canvas and fabric match, then make lines of basting diagonally in both directions and around sides of canvas. The design is then worked by making crosses as shown, taking each stitch diagonally over the double mesh of canvas and through the fabric, being careful not to catch the canvas.

When the design is completed, the basting is removed and the horizontal threads of the canvas are carefully drawn out, one strand at a time, then the vertical threads, leaving the finished cross-stitch design on the fabric.

Penelope canvas is available in several size meshes. Choose finer sizes for smaller designs; larger sizes are suitable for coarse work in wool.

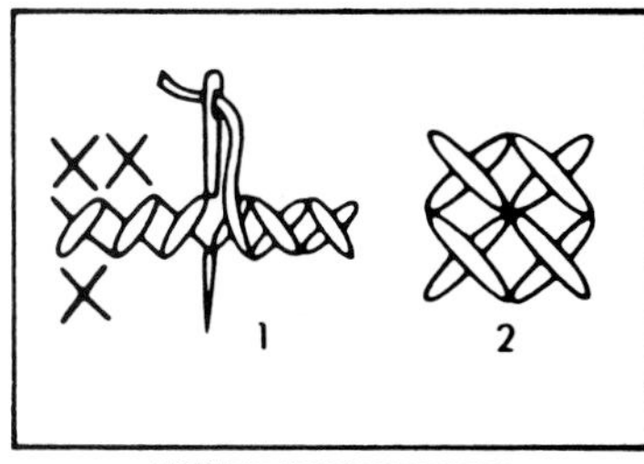

HOW TO MAKE CROSSES

Embroidery Stitch Details

BACKSTITCH

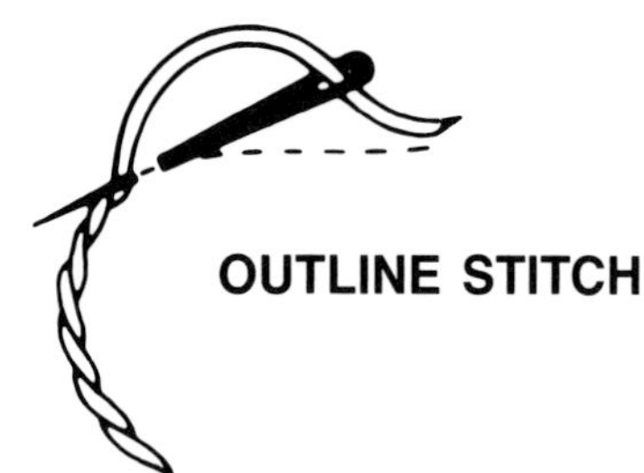

OUTLINE STITCH

RUNNING STITCH

STRAIGHT STITCH

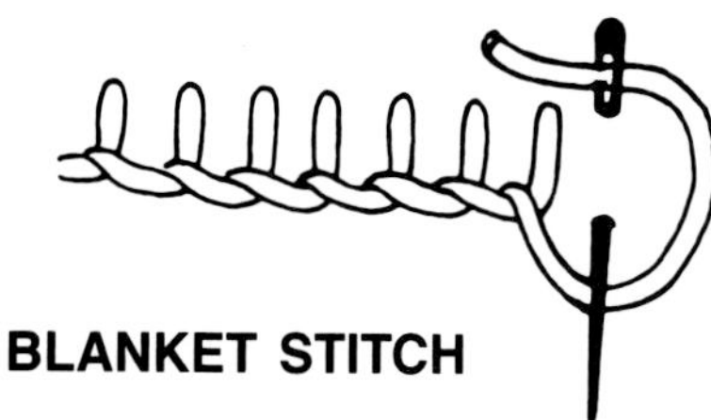

BLANKET STITCH

HALF CROSS-STITCH

FRENCH KNOT

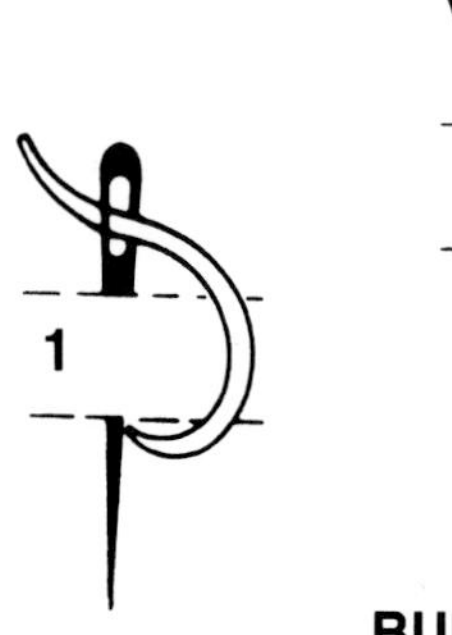

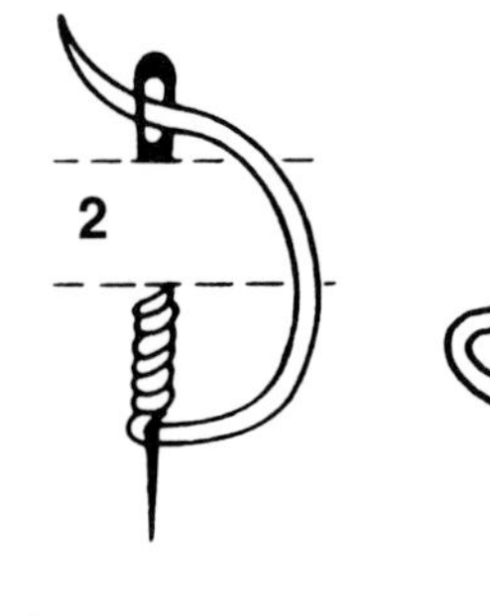

BULLION STITCH

LAZY DAISY

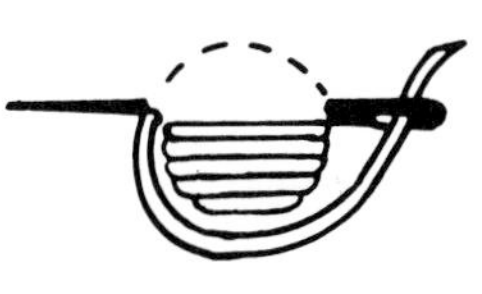

SATIN STITCH

PADDED SATIN STITCH

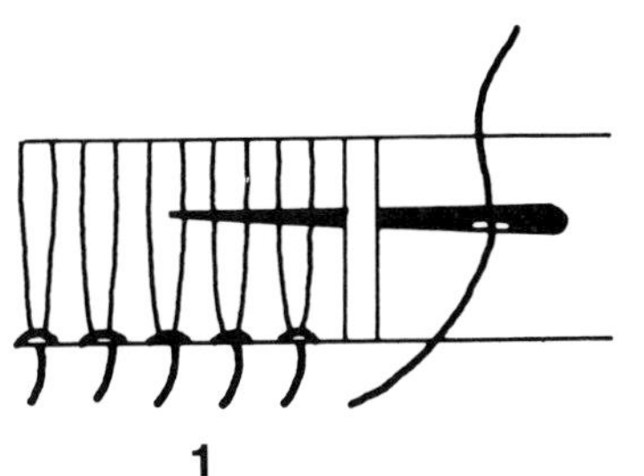

1

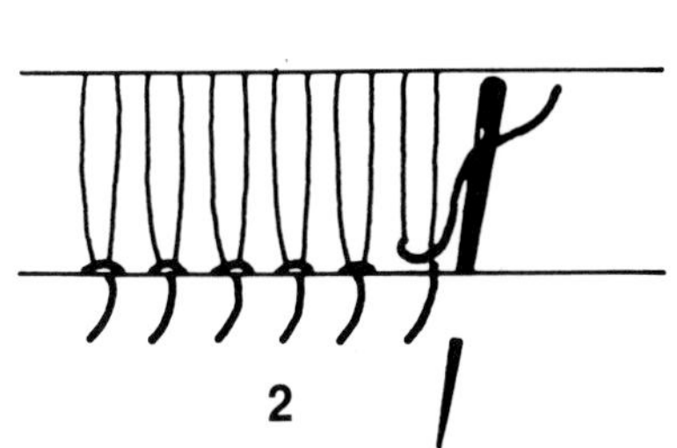

2

HEMSTITCHING

How to Make a Twisted Cord

Method requires two people. Tie one end of yarn around pencil. Loop yarn over center of second pencil, back to and around first, and back to second, making as many strands between pencils as needed for thickness of cord; knot end to pencil. Length of yarn between pencils should be three times length of cord desired. Each person holds yarn just below pencil with one hand and twists pencil with other hand, keeping yarn taut. When yarn begins to kink, catch center over doorknob or back of chair. Bring pencils together for one person to hold, while other grasps center of yarn, sliding hand down and releasing at short intervals, letting yarn twist to form cord.

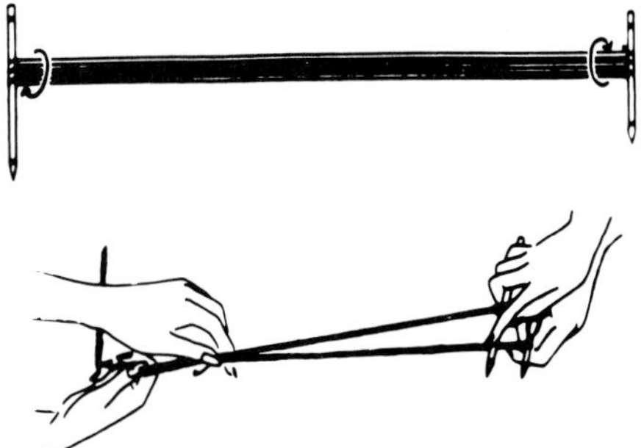

How to Do Hardanger Embroidery

Kloster Blocks

(See charts A and B, page 48)

Thread tapestry needle with a 36″ length of size 5 pearl cotton. Bring needle to right side of cloth at pin, leaving a 2″ length at back; work first stitches over end to secure. Beginning at arrow, work first block, stitching five satin stitches over four fabric threads as shown on project chart. Following chart, continue to make blocks, working in a counterclockwise direction back to starting point. Parallel blocks have four threads between them; perpendicular blocks share a hole of the fabric. To begin and end threads, return needle to wrong side and run it under threads of last block made; bring needle back over last two threads and slip it under them again, then run needle under several more blocks. Never end thread in middle of a block.

Woven Bars

Weave each group of four threads between open squares, using a 36″ length of size 8 pearl cotton or two strands of floss in tapestry needle. For each group, anchor thread end under nearby Kloster blocks; bring needle to front at edge of thread area to be woven. Slip needle down through center of thread area, with two threads on either side of needle, then up at opposite edge (**Fig. 1**). Bring needle to wrong side through center and repeat this figure-8 motion across threads until they are covered (**Fig. 2**). See details below for finished bar. Keep tension of the working thread snug and even throughout weaving. To move to next group, go diagonally across a corner on wrong side. To move to another column, slip needle under backs of Kloster blocks.

Dove's Eyes

Work dove's eyes in the open squares marked by X's or diamonds on project charts. Thread needle with same thread used for woven bars; anchor thread at center of a Kloster block or bar, on wrong side. Bring needle to right side through square, then insert it into center of an adjoining Kloster block or bar (**Fig. 1**). Leaving thread rather slack, bring needle up into open square, crossing over stitch made, and insert into the next block or bar (**Fig. 2**). Repeat in next block or bar (**Fig. 3**), then go under the first stitch made and through block or bar at starting point (**Fig. 4**). Move thread between squares as for bars.

WOVEN BARS

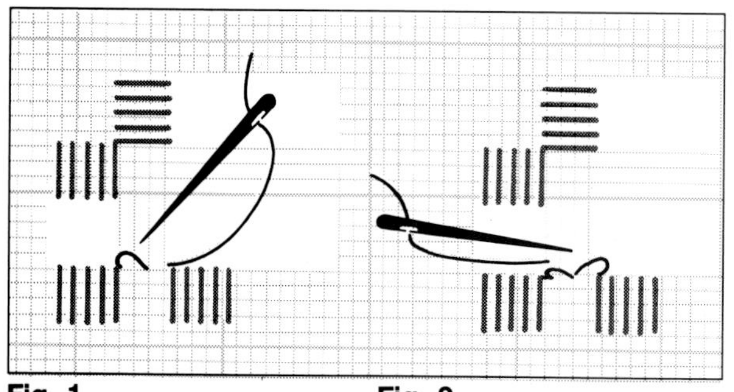

Fig. 1 Fig. 2

DOVE'S EYES

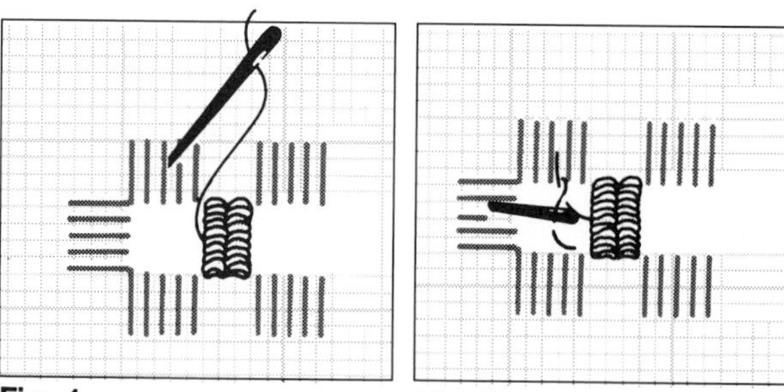

Fig. 1 Fig. 2

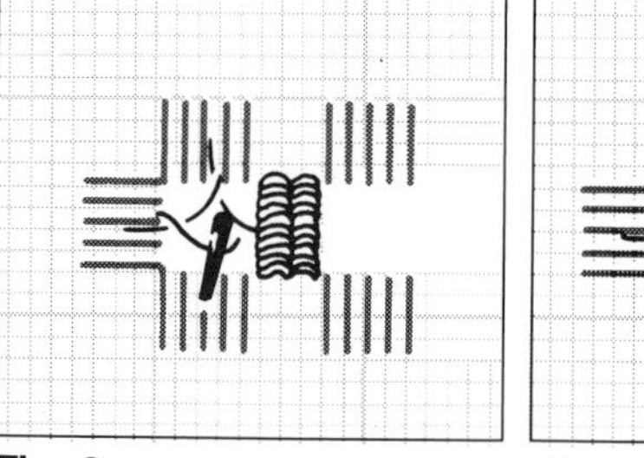

Fig. 3

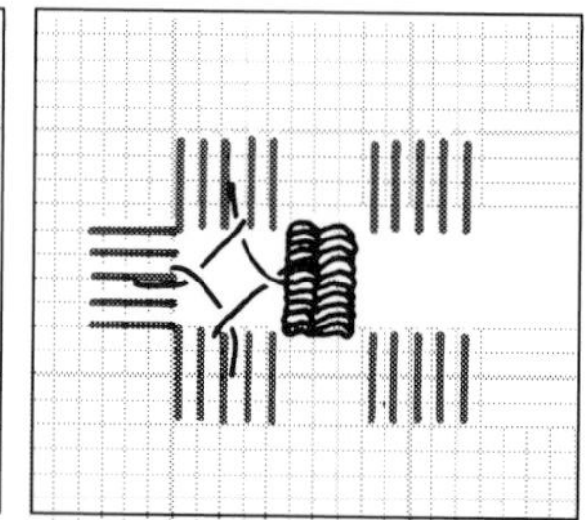

Fig. 4

Sewing Hints

To Join Fabric Pieces: Pin pieces together with right sides facing each other and raw edges even, unless otherwise directed. Machine-stitch on marked lines with matching thread, making ¼″ seams unless otherwise directed; ease in any fullness where necessary. When assembling clothes, press seams open after stitching, unless otherwise specified. When joining patch pieces, press seams to one side, under darker color. Do not press vinyl, fur, or napped fabrics unless otherwise directed. Clip into seam allowance at curves and across corners; turn piece to right side when directed and poke out corners with knitting needle. Assemble and finish pieces as directed, referring to color photograph.

To Make a Hem: Press fabric edge ¼″ to wrong side. Turn under again to desired depth; press. Topstitch by machine or slip-stitch by hand.

To Attach Lace Trim: For Finished Fabric Edges: Press fabric edge ¼″ to wrong side. For flat edge (such as sleeve or leg bottom not yet assembled), cut lace to fit folded edge. For continuous edge (such as hem for assembled skirt or around a place mat), cut lace same length as fold, plus ½″. Pin lace to fabric, overlapping edges ⅛″-¼″ on right or wrong side as directed and with finished edge of lace extending beyond fabric; for continuous edge, also overlap lace ends ½″. Stitch lace in place.

Enclosing Lace in Seams: Cut lace same length as fabric edge, unless otherwise directed. Pin lace to one fabric piece with right sides facing and raw edges even. Pin second fabric piece over first one, right sides facing and sandwiching lace between fabric layers. Stitch ¼″ from pinned edge through all three layers. Turn piece to right side; lace will extend beyond seam.

To Make a Pillow: Cut out pillow front from fabric, needlepoint canvas, felt, etc., as specified. Cut pillow back same size. If desired, add ruffle or welting as directed below, then assemble pillow: Stitch pillow front and back together, making ½″ seams and leaving an opening in one side for turning. Turn pillow to right side. Stuff firmly with fiberfill, or insert pillow form. Turn in raw edges and slip-stitch opening closed.

For Ruffle: Cut fabric strip for ruffle as directed, piecing together as necessary. Stitch ruffle ends together; press seam open. Fold ruffle in half lengthwise, right side out; press. Using a long basting stitch, gather ruffle ½″ from raw edges to fit around pillow front. Stitch ruffle to right side of pillow front.

Patchwork How-To's

To Make Patchwork Templates: Draw and label patterns on graph paper, using ruler to mark straight lines; do not cut out yet. Glue paper pattern to cardboard; let dry. Cut out on marked lines, for templates.

To Mark Patch Pieces: Place template on wrong side of fabric with parallel edges, right angles, or one straight edge on straight grain. Mark around template with sharp pencil held at an outward angle. Mark specified number of pieces needed on one fabric at one time, leaving ½″ between pieces.

To Cut Pattern/Patchwork Pieces: Cut out fabric pieces ¼″ beyond marked lines (stitching lines) for seam allowance, unless otherwise directed. If cutting additional pieces without patterns, do not add seam allowance; it is included in dimensions given. To prevent knit-backed or loosely woven fabric from raveling, zigzag stitch all raw edges as necessary.

Piecing: To join two patch pieces by hand, place them together, right sides facing, matching angles and marked lines; pin. Thread a sharp needle with an 18″ length of sewing thread. Begin with a small knot, then stitch along marked seam line with tiny running stitches, ending with a few backstitches. Try to make 8 to 10 running stitches per inch. As you join pieces, press seams to one side; open seams tend to weaken construction.

To join pieces by machine, set machine for 10 stitches per inch and join as for hand piecing.

Quilting

Assembly: Cut backing and batting same size as quilt top, unless otherwise directed. Place backing, wrong side up, on large, flat surface. Place batting on backing and smooth out any bumps or wrinkles. Before adding quilt top, baste batting to lining by taking two long stitches in a cross. Place quilt top on batting, right side up. Pin all layers together to hold temporarily, using large safety pins. Baste generously through all thicknesses, using a sturdy thread and large needle: Baste on the lengthwise and crosswise grain of the fabric, then baste diagonally across in two directions and around sides, top, and bottom.

Quilting Stitch: Cut 18″ strand of thread. Knot one end. Bring needle up from lining through quilt top; give a little tug to thread so that knot passes through lining only and lies buried in batting. Sew on marked line with running stitch, making stitches as small and close as you can (5–10 per inch); space stitches evenly, so they are the same length on both sides of quilt. To end off, backstitch and take a long stitch through the top and batting only; take another backstitch and clip thread at surface; the thread end will sink into batting.

Start in the middle of the quilt and stitch toward you; shift your position as you work, so that the quilting progresses fairly evenly on all sides toward the outside of the quilt.

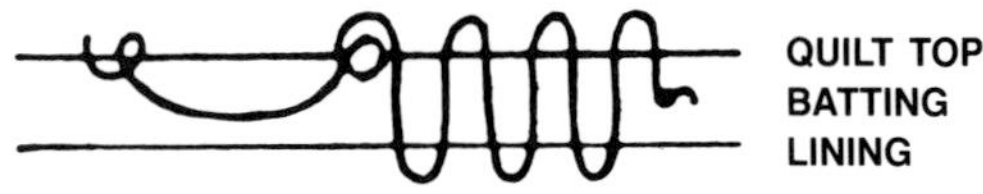

To Miter Corners: Sew border pieces to quilt top, with an equal amount extending at each end, for corners. Lay quilt top flat, right side down. Hold adjacent ends of border pieces together at corners with right sides facing. Keeping border flat, lift up inner corners and pin strips together diagonally from inner corners to outer corners; baste, then stitch, on basting line. Cut off excess fabric to make ¼″ seam; press seam open.

A MITERED CORNER

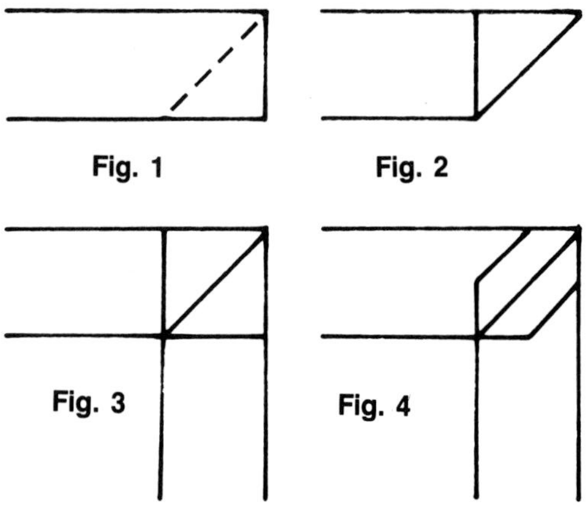

Fig. 1

Fig. 2

Fig. 3

Fig. 4

Index